£22.95

R54148

D1447713

WITHDRAWN FROM STOCK

WHERE'S MY SPACE AGE?

Sean Topham

WHERE'S MY SPACE AGE?

The rise and fall of futuristic design

Munich • Berlin • London • New York

For Gemma, Rhiannon, Polly, James and Samuel

© for the text by Sean Topham
© for design and layout by Prestel Verlag, Munich · Berlin · London · New York 2003
© for illustrations see Picture Credits, page 160
The right of Sean Topham to be identified as author of this work has been asserted in accordance with the Copyright, Designs and Patents Act 1988.

Front cover, top to bottom, left to right: see pp. 27, 35, 124, 63, 79, 106, 26, 130, © Robert Opie (toy spacecraft), 72, 22
Back cover, top to bottom, left to right: see pp. 21, 146, 7, 121, 128, 33, 145
Frontispiece: In a 1952 series of articles written in *Collier's*, Wernher von Braun, wrote of a large wheel-like space station in a 1,730-km orbit. This concept was illustrated by artist Chesley Bonestell.

Prestel Verlag
Königinstrasse 9,
D-80539 Munich
Tel. +49 (89) 38 17 09-0
Fax +49 (89) 38 17 09-35
www.prestel.de

Prestel Publishing Ltd.
4, Bloomsbury Place,
London WC1A 2QA
Tel. +44 (020) 7323 5004
Fax +44 (020) 7636 8004

Prestel Publishing
175 Fifth Avenue, Suite 402,
New York, N.Y. 10010
Tel. +1 (212) 995-2720
Fax +1 (212) 995-2733
www.prestel.com

Library of Congress Control Number: 2002116860

The Deutsche Bibliothek holds a record of this publication in the Deutsche Nationalbibliographie; detailed bibliographical data can be found under: http://dnb.dde.de

Prestel books are available worldwide. Please contact your nearest bookseller or one of the above addresses for information concerning your local distributor.

Editorial direction: Philippa Hurd
Design, layout, and typesetting: sugarfreedesign, London, Tel +44(0)20 7243 2100
Origination: Kestrel Digital Colour, England
Printing: Passavia, Passau
Binding: Conzella, Pfarrkirchen

Printed in Germany on acid-free paper.

ISBN 3-7913-2844-1

Author's Acknowledgments
In addition to all the contributors who made this book possible my particular thanks are due to all the folks at sugarfreedesign and the staff at the National Art Library in the V&A Museum. I'd also like to say a big thank you to all my friends and family for their continuing support and good wishes, and finally, an extra big thank you to Sally Rickaby, without whom none of this would be possible.

00 Contents

Right: Chesley Bonestell, *Rocket to the Moon*, as featured on the cover of *Mechanix Illustrated*, September 1945.

01 "I took a trip on a Gemini spacecraft"

"I like rockets of all kinds," said a twelve-year-old Michigan boy on the eve of the lunar landing in 1969. "I'd like to be an astronaut. It sounds like a pretty good job to me. Good pay and you find something new every time you go up." His words echo the sentiments of many children growing up in the first decade of space travel, their fascination fuelled by comics and confectionery, rayguns and robots, modules and capsules—all of which held out the promise of an exciting space-age future. I was only two months old when the astronauts Eugene Cernan and Harrison Schmitt, the last astronauts to walk on the moon, blasted off from the lunar surface in December 1972. As a child growing up in the 1970s I was well aware of the moon landings and, like many others at the time, believed it to be only the start of an exciting new era: the space age.

Space travel has always been a reality in my lifetime. Only two decades prior to the first lunar landing in 1969, however, the conquest of space had seemed a distant fantasy: stories of the intergalactic exploits of Dan Dare, Flash Gordon, and Rick Random were always set in a far-off future. But it was not long before those fictional heroes were joined by the real thing. In the 1950s a serious debate about the onset of the space age caught the public's imagination. Voyages into outer space had long been used in works of fiction to thrill, inspire, and threaten. Authors such as Cyrano de Bergerac in *Voyage to the Moon and Sun* (1656), and Voltaire in *Micromegas* (1752), used the fantasy of space

Top: Two comics and a story-book from an era when space travel was still regarded as a far-off fantasy.

travel to satirize the realities of life on earth. Jules Verne, H.G. Wells, and many others continued this tradition into the 20th century.

Arthur C. Clarke's *The Exploration of Space* (1951), however, was not a work of fiction. It was an accurate description of how interplanetary travel was likely to evolve over the next few decades. Space travel was about to shift from fiction to reality. As Clarke himself remarked, "in what might be called its 'classic form' the space travel story will soon disappear, for history is overtaking imagination." The successes of Clarke's book and Willy Ley's work *Rockets, Missiles and Space Travel* (1950) were clear indications of the public's appetite for astronautics. It was Clarke's specific intention with *The Exploration of Space* to demystify the complexities of interplanetary travel and deliver the subject to a wider audience. As chairman of the British Interplanetary Society his serious treatment of the subject was brought to life in vivid illustrations by the artist R.A. Smith. Smith made every attempt in the conception of his images to "avoid mere fantasy" and provide detailed renderings of spacecraft that were as realistic as possible. While Clarke was adept at describing the rockets that might one day propel people into space, Smith's drawings served as inspiration to laymen and specialists alike and fed a desire for images which would define the approaching space age. Indeed the spacecraft Smith depicted in the drawings *High-altitude Man-carrying Rocket* and *Lunar-type Spaceship* bear a striking similarity to the vessels used in the 1960s.

Popular interest in space travel certainly provided an exciting distraction at a time when the recent past was too dreadful to contemplate. After the misery and destruction of World War II there was a strong desire for change and intense optimism for the future. The Festival of Britain shot up from the wartime ruins on London's South Bank and was a positive celebration of things to come. The exhibition's centerpiece was the flying-saucer-shaped Dome of Discovery and beside it stood the rocket-like beacon, Skylon. However, the dreams and imaginings of a space-age utopia were soon to be eclipsed by the real thing.

The space age came roaring out of the political hostility between the United States of America and the Union of Soviet Socialist Republics. From the start of the Cold War these bitter rivals had wrestled with rocket science in a battle for international prestige and superiority in space. The era witnessed unrivalled technical achievement on both sides of the Iron Curtain. Its

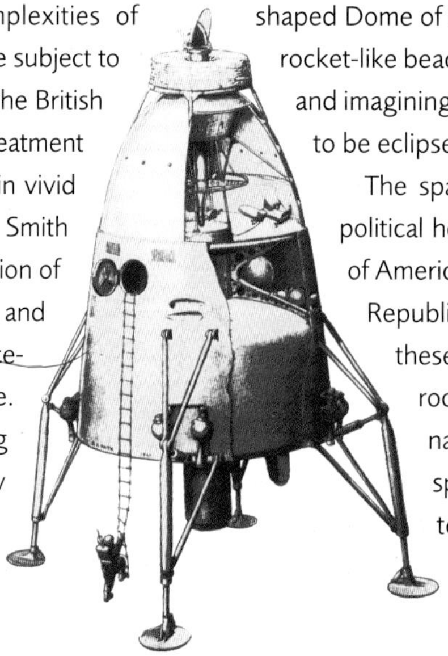

Top left: Soviet cigarette box, early 1960s.

Top right: Dan Dare Cosmic Ray Gun. 1950s' toys like these helped generate excitement in children for space travel, while older minds were stimulated by artists such as R.A. Smith.

Right: R.A. Smith, *Lunar-type Spaceship: Sectional View.*

impact was astounding and the whole planet seemed to go crazy for the cosmos.

Warming up in the red corner was the Soviet Union and its mysteriously anonymous Chief Designer (the identity of this shadowy figure behind the Soviet space program remained a closely guarded secret until after his death). Limbering up in the blue corner was the United States and its superstar rocket scientist, Wernher von Braun. The USSR and the USA had a strong background in rocket science: the Soviets with the theoretical work of Konstantin Tsiolkovsky, and the Americans with the rocketry experiments of physicist Robert Goddard. Since the end of World War II, however, both superpowers profited from research conducted by German scientists working for Adolf Hitler: the Chief Designer had a number of captured German scientists at his disposal while Wernher von Braun, who was apprehended by the Americans to develop missiles for the US Army, had been the key figure behind Hitler's terrifying V2 missile.

Von Braun quickly achieved celebrity status in the USA and was even featured on the cover of *Time* magazine, who dubbed him "astronaut von Braun". The magazine often ran features that looked to the future and the possibilities of space travel, and in 1951 it devoted a cover to a space-walking robot and asked the question, "Will Man Outgrow the Earth?" In the early 1950s, magazines such as *Life* and *Time* helped generate anticipation amongst the American public for a future dominated by the conquest of space.

Wernher von Braun, like Arthur C. Clarke and R. A. Smith, was quick to acknowledge the power of images in conveying his theories of rocket propulsion and space travel. He contributed his scientific propositions on several occasions to the popular magazine *Collier's*. It was for these articles that the artist Chesley Bonestell collaborated with von Braun, providing dramatic pictures to accompany von Braun's pioneering texts. Bonestell was already well known for his space-inspired illustrations, which appeared in magazines such as *Mechanix Illustrated*. The images he created with von Braun, like those by R. A. Smith, stand as accurate renditions of the earliest vessels with the potential to travel in space. The first of von Braun's *Collier's* articles appeared in March 1952, and the cover of that issue featured a Bonestell painting beneath the headline: "Man Will Conquer Space Soon". As von Braun rose to prominence, the ideas he put forward in *Collier's* set the agenda for America's journeys into space.

Much to the surprise of the rest of the world it was the Soviets who threw the first punch in this

Above: R.A. Smith, *High-altitude Man-carrying Rocket*. Smith joined the British Interplanetary Society in 1937 and shortly after World War II became a designer at the Ministry of Supply's Rocket Research Establishment.

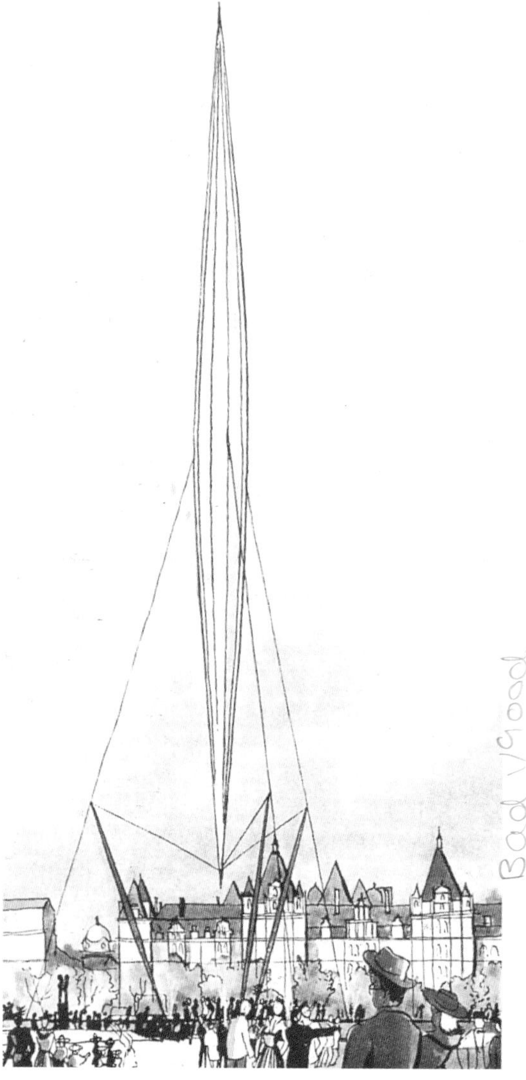

Top: Artist's impression of the futuristic Dome of Discovery at the Festival of Britain, 1951. Inside visitors were able to watch the return of radar impulses beamed from the adjacent Skylon (right) and reflected from the surface of the moon.

titanic bout. On October 4, 1957, the USSR launched Prostreishiy Sputnik [Simple Satellite] scoring a significant victory with this polished aluminum sphere, which measured 57 cm in diameter and weighed 83 kg. The act of catapulting that small metallic sphere into orbit sent shockwaves around the earth and signalled the arrival of the space age. The Soviet news agency, Tass, wired an announcement to the world's press shortly after the Sputnik launch, and the news broke in Washington during a timely reception for American officials and journalists at the Soviet Embassy. It was a huge propaganda coup for the USSR and the headlines across the *New York Times* the next morning read: "Soviet Fires Earth Satellite into Space; it is Circling the Globe at 18,000 mph; Sphere Tracked in Four Crossings over US."

In the West the reaction was mixed: initial amazement among the American scientific community was soon tempered with fear and alarm in political and military circles. If the USSR had the capacity to launch a satellite into space then it also had the ability to fire a nuclear missile at the United States. The direct relationship between space exploration and missile development explains in part why the onset of the space age provoked such contrasting reactions of amazement and fear.

While politicians and military leaders exploited feelings of unease, toy manufacturers capitalized on

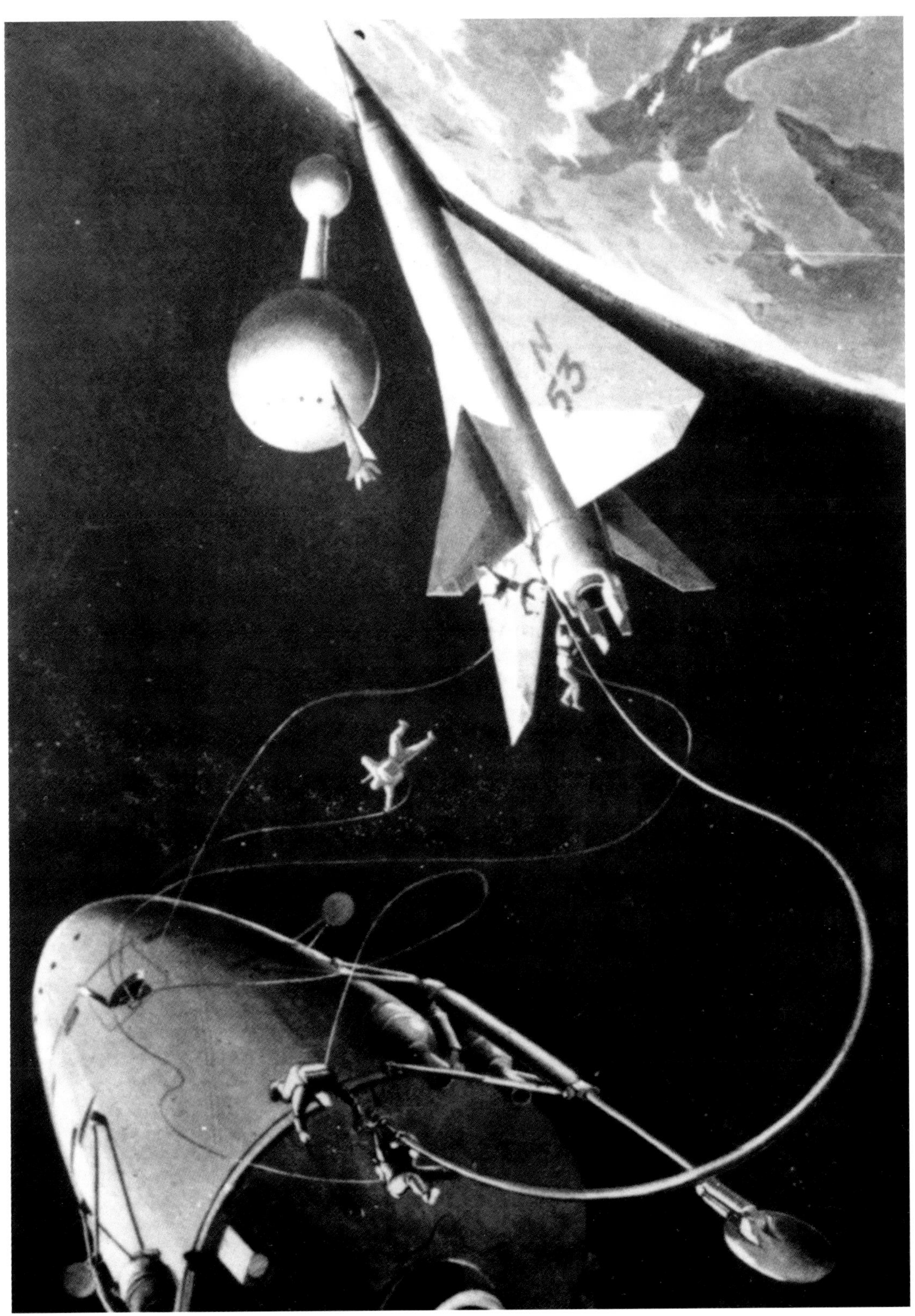

Left: R.A. Smith, *Spaceships Refuelling in Free Orbit*. Another of Smith's convincing illustrations from Arthur C. Clarke's *The Exploration of Space*, 1951.

DAILY EXPRESS

No. 17,844 SATURDAY OCTOBER 5 1957 Price 2d.

Midnight—and London hears the first signals

SPACE AGE IS HERE

MOSCOW RADIO ANNOUNCES:

Man-made moon is circling world in 95 minutes

By CHAPMAN PINCHER

MAN entered the Space Age yesterday when Russia rocketed an earth satellite—a man-made moon—into outer space. It is now circling the world 560 miles up once every 95 minutes.

An announcement from Tass, the Soviet News Agency, said the satellite—about 23 inches in diameter and weighing about 184lb.—could be seen in the rays of the rising and setting sun with ordinary binoculars or spy glasses.

WHY, LOOK WHO'S HERE!

Mrs. Mike Parker names woman

Married in 1943

THAT 7%

WILSON: I've evidence leak was political

MACMILLAN: I'll act if you prove it

By TREVOR EVANS

MR. HAROLD WILSON said last night that he has definite evidence of a political leak over the Bank rate—and at once the Prime Minister intervened personally in the row and said that if Mr. Wilson produces the evidence it will go before the Lord Chancellor.

Warsaw rioters stone police

NIGHT No. 2

the public's sense of amazement. Spacecraft were no longer just fantasy playthings dreamed up by model makers: they were real and one was now circling the earth, the first of many. The space age began to infiltrate the home as tin replicas of the Sputnik satellite appeared in stores and miniature "spinning sputniks" were given away free in cereal packets. Quaker recommended its Puffed Wheat as the ideal breakfast cereal to "launch big and little spacemen" at the start of every day. Promotional packets of the cereal included a "two-color plastic sputnik", which could be catapulted into orbit with an elastic band and promised "sure fire fun for children."

Another toy to celebrate the satellite's success was the Spitnik, which used a water pump to send it into orbit around the backyard. These toys generated even more excitement about the arrival of the space age —the message was out that the new era was going to be thrilling and fun. Ironically these novelties, produced for the western consumer, were inspired by Soviet advances in the space race.

While the White House and the Pentagon were still reeling with shock at the first satellite launch, the Russians struck again. On November 3, 1957, to coincide with the fortieth anniversary of the October revolution, the USSR launched Sputnik 2. This time the satellite carried a passenger: on board, and much to the indignation of the British public, was Laika the cosmonaut dog. She was there to prove that life could be sustained in zero gravity but animal lovers in Britain were outraged at the experiment and made their feelings known to the Soviet Embassy in London. Laika was the first earthling to travel into space but sadly she did not complete the return journey alive. In the first of many bizarre pop-cultural tributes to the space age Laika's personal sacrifice was commemorated by a Russian tobacco company who introduced a new brand of cigarettes and named it in her honor. Soviet citizens could now smoke their way into the space age with the new Laika cigarettes, and the cigarettes could even be stored in a Sputnik-shaped dispenser and stubbed out in a matching ashtray. Laika cigarettes demonstrate that it was not only children who were captivated by the arrival of space travel: adults, too, were being sold the idea that the new space age was going to change their everyday lives.

Sputnik 2 dealt a

Top right: Newspapers the world over were quick to announce the launch of Sputnik 1 and the arrival of the space age.

Right and top left: Late 1950s' toys such as the Spitnik and Spinning Sputnik promoted the notion that the space age was going to be fun.

second crushing blow to the pride of the USA and the pressure was on President Eisenhower to match the Soviet achievement. The world's press focused its attention on the US Navy's launch facility at Cape Canaveral, Florida in December 1957. After numerous delays and complications the American Vanguard rocket was ignited. Its mission was to launch a small satellite into orbit, but the rocket exploded on its pad and the satellite plopped back to earth. The official news release stated: "Exploded—no casualties" but the headline splashed across the following morning's London *Daily Herald* read, "Oh what a flopnik!" The United States had failed to enter the space age where the Soviet Union had succeeded—twice. To make matters worse the American satellite was tiny, measuring only 15 cm in diameter and weighing only 1.36 kg, not much bigger than a grapefruit. The whole fiasco was lambasted by members of Congress, and Soviet delegates at the United Nations caused further embarrassment by asking if the USA might benefit from the technical assistance Moscow was handing out to "backward" nations.

Left: Dr. Wernher von Braun at his desk beside models of the rockets that would later be used to send astronauts into space. Hanging on the wall behind him is an illustration of his proposal for a moonlander spacecraft.

here's my space age?

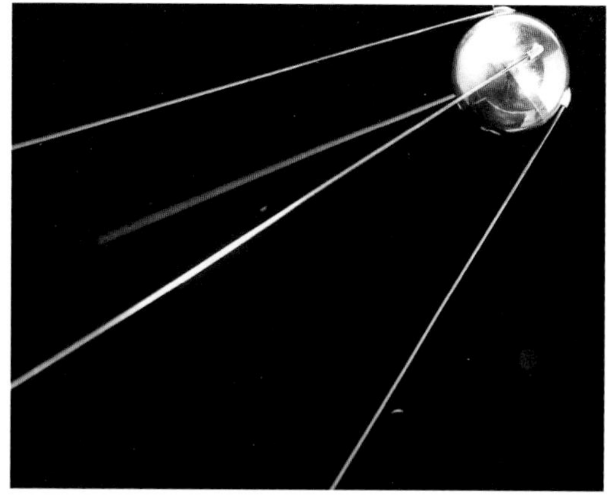

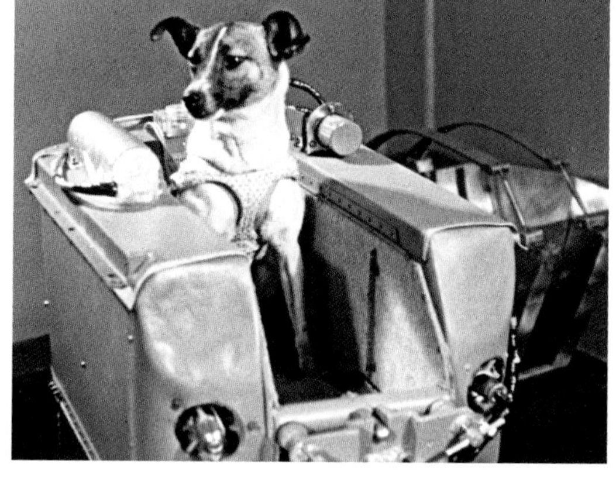

The US Navy's Vanguard rocket failed to launch on several further occasions. In a desperate bid to save face, it was decided that the army and Wernher von Braun should step in with the Jupiter-C rocket and Explorer 1 satellite. Von Braun's rocket, despite being more reliable, had initially been rejected because it was designed to carry a warhead and the United States government were concerned that its launch might be perceived as an act of aggression. However, now that the USA was seen to be trailing behind the USSR, all such thoughts were abandoned. The Jupiter-C rocket blasted off and carried the Explorer 1 satellite into orbit on January, 31, 1958, almost four months after the launch of Sputnik 1. Relief spread quickly across the United States and in Huntsville, Alabama, where the Jupiter rocket was made, a jubilant crowd gathered with banners reading "Space Is Ours" and "Flopnik Now Hitnik". America had finally entered the space age, and after a faltering start the battle to conquer space had begun.

When the Chief Designer launched Laika the dog into space it was a clear sign that the Soviet Union ultimately intended to send a human into orbit. In response the Americans committed themselves to long-term space exploration in October, 1958 with the inauguration of the National Aeronautics and Space Administration (NASA). This non-military agency was assigned the task of coordinating the United States' attack on outer space. One of its first assignments was to recruit some real life spacemen.

The first seven superstars of the space age were introduced to the world at a NASA press conference on April 9, 1959. These astronauts brought a human dimension to space travel and became heroes for a generation of youngsters across the USA. The seven men were: Alan B. Shepard, Virgil "Gus" Grissom, L. Gordon Cooper, Walter M. Schirra, Donald "Deke" Slayton, John Glenn, and M. Scott Carpenter, all regular-looking guys who would eventually perform some very irregular feats. Their names became legendary and kids everywhere wanted to grow up and become one of them.

Aside from the proposed manned missions there was plenty of action still to be had in space. While the American government made preparations for the first visit of a Soviet leader, the Chief Designer prepared another well-timed propaganda victory for the USSR. Khrushchev's visit was preceded by the Soviet probe, Luna 2, thundering into space and crashing into the moon. To underline the capture of

Top left: Sputnik I, the Soviet satellite that started the space age.

Right and top right: Laika, the doomed cosmonaut dog, and the cigarette brand that was launched in her honor.

Left: "Oh what a flopnik!". The US Navy's Vanguard rocket exploding on its launch pad.

Right: The tiny Vanguard satellite SLV-2, a later version of the satellite that heaped embarrassment on the United States' government after its failed launch in December, 1957. The SLV-2 was launched in June, 1958, but its mission was also prematurely terminated due to a fault in the launch vehicle.

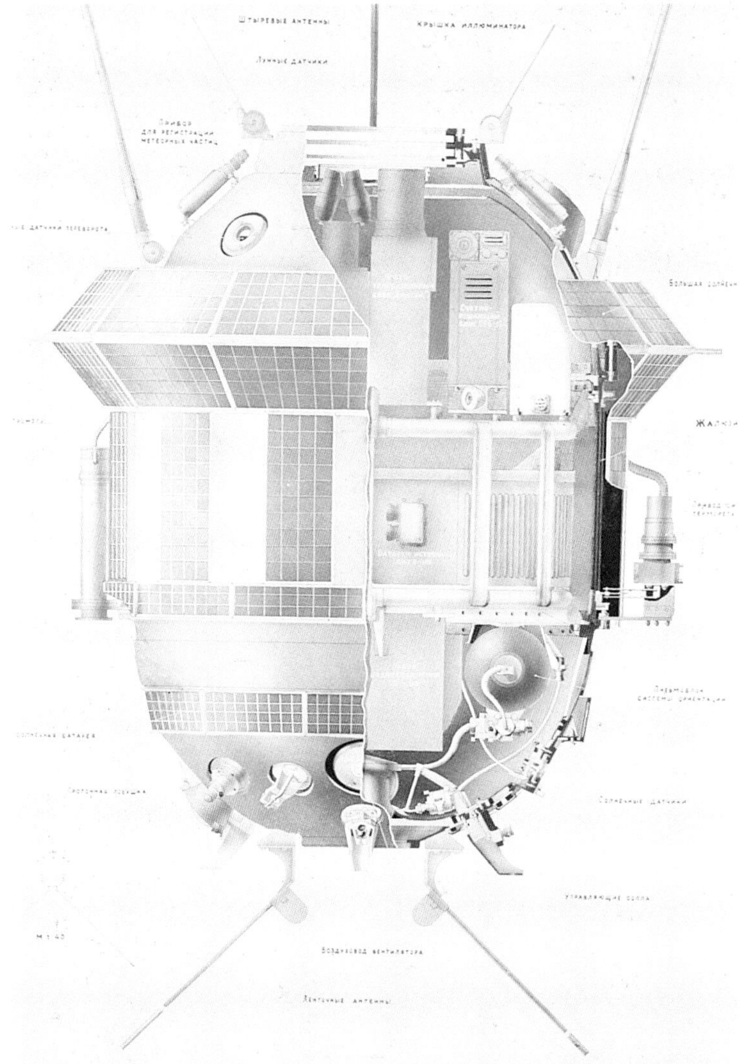

Left: Diagrammatic of Luna 3, the first satellite to photograph the far side of the moon, launched October 4, 1959.

territory, as the probe hit the lunar surface a pennant bearing the emblem of the Soviet Union shot out to stake the Russian claim. Back in Moscow, thousands of Russians lined the pathways outside the city's planetarium to take turns in looking through fifteen telescopes that had been specially erected for the lunar landing. Loudspeakers carrying crucial broadcasts were set up in other Moscow parks, which remained open so that the people could party late into the night. The Russians had reason to celebrate again less than a month later when Luna 3 —in what was a truly remarkable feat for the time—became the first spacecraft to send back photographs of the dark side of the moon. Thus the USSR and its Chief Designer had landed the first punches in the earliest rounds of the contest for space. These victories helped alter the international perception of a country that was often in the news for the wrong reasons, while also casting doubt over the technological prowess of the United States.

But despite early setbacks, the USA was beginning to reap the benefits of its methodical

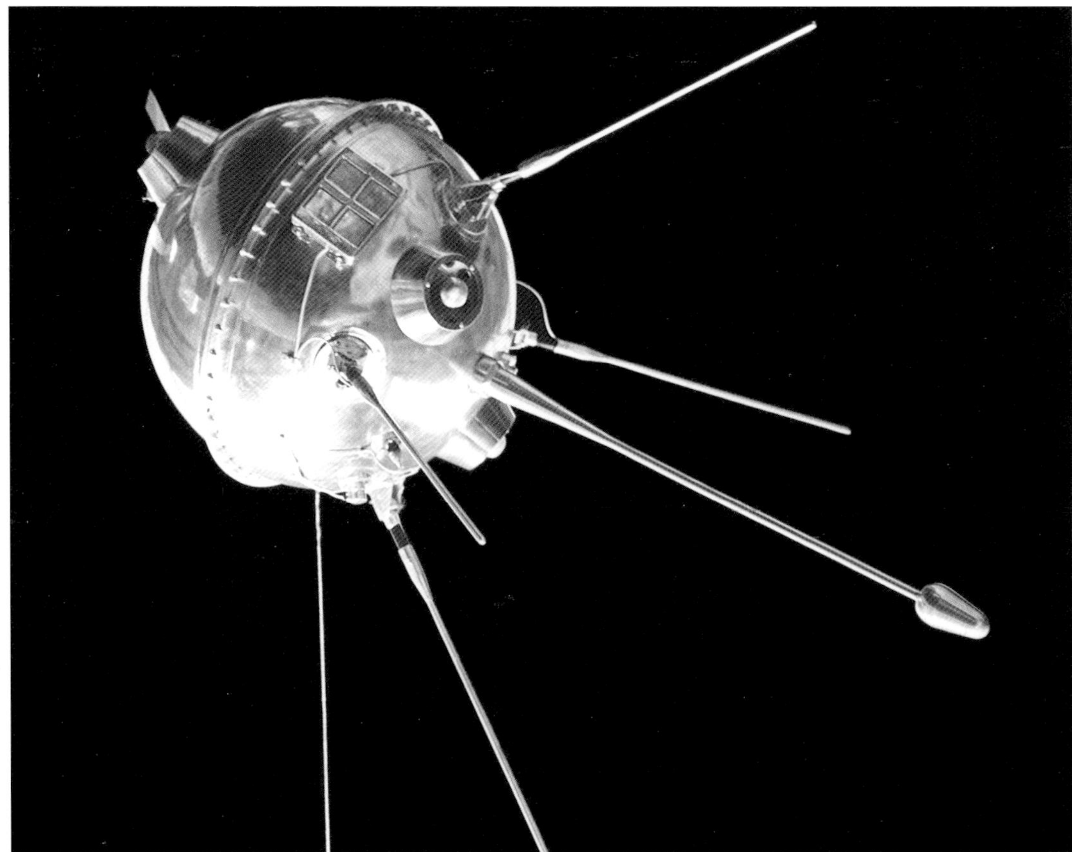

Top: Soviet satellite Luna 2, launched September, 1959, was the first man-made object to reach the moon.

Right: Moscow citizens in a city park observing Luna 2 following its lunar touchdown.

approach to space travel and was about to score a first of its own. In August 1960, the Echo 1 satellite—a giant inflated sphere made with aluminized Mylar film—became the first satellite to serve the needs of private industry. The massive reflective sphere was used to bounce radio signals between different stations on earth and so became the first true communications satellite. The crucial size and weight restrictions of launch vehicle payload bays forced spacecraft designers to consider new ways of packing down equipment. Echo 1 was inflatable, which meant it occupied only a small capacity on the journey into space and, once ejected, was able to expand to its full size. Bell laboratories developed Echo 1 for the AT&T company and, in so doing, marked the emergence of commercial enterprise in outer space. The descendents of Echo 1 now beam all kinds of signals into the home, however, in the early 1960s, it was the first astronauts who delivered the space age into the domestic environment.

The seven NASA astronauts quickly reached celebrity status in the USA and the rest of the world. Their pictures were all over the press, they were used to endorse products from cameras to cars, and they even appeared on television chat shows. The astronauts brought a human face to the space age. Satellites were complex scientific instruments: they could send back photographs and radio signals but they could not express how it actually felt to be in space. The astronauts also brought some much needed humor to the proceedings and comedians began to introduce astronaut themes into their routines. Perhaps the best known of these was comedian Bill Dana's character, "Jose Jimenez—the reluctant astronaut." Jose first appeared on American television as an act on the Garry Moore Show in early 1960. The real astronauts later mimicked his lines in radio communications between their capsules and ground control. Dana released a novelty single featuring Jose Jimenez in 1961 through Kapp records, and the cover showed the terrified face of the reluctant astronaut as he was launched into space. Astronaut Alan Shepard was a big fan and

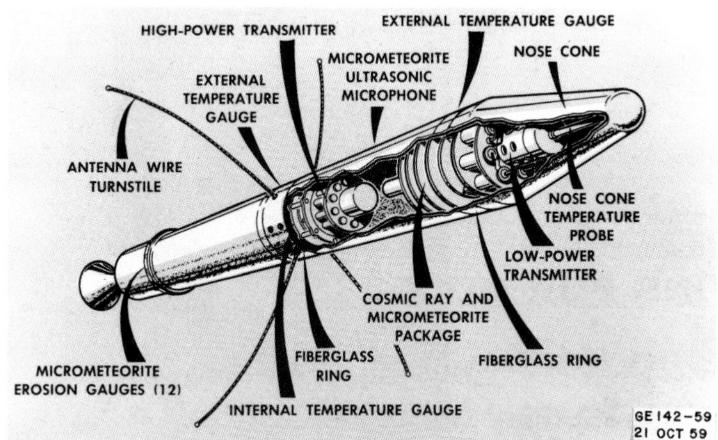

Top: Cutaway illustration of Explorer I, America's first successful satellite. Launched on January 31, 1958, it discovered the Van Allen Radiation Belt that surrounds the Earth.

Right: Test inflation of the Bell Laboratories' Echo I satellite in a blimp hangar at Weeksville, North Carolina. This enormous inflated sphere was the first commercial satellite and instigated a revolution in communications technology.

Left: Project Mercury astronauts, whose selection was announced on April 9, 1959. Front row, left to right, Walter M. Schirra, Jr., Donald K. Slayton, John H. Glenn, Jr., and M. Scott Carpenter; back row, Alan B. Shepard, Jr. Virgil I. "Gus" Grissom, and L. Gordon Cooper.

LIFE

EXCLUSIVE ON MEN PICKED FOR SPACE

ASTRONAUT FIRST TEAM

GLENN, GRISSOM SHEPARD

REG. U. S. PAT. OFF.

MARCH 3, 1961 20 CENTS

Right and **opposite:** *Life* magazine held the exclusive rights to cover the private lives of all the Mercury astronauts. This feature describes Glenn as "an unswerving and a self-denying man engaged in a dangerous pursuit", Shepard as "a cool customer and a hot pilot with an eye for the big picture", and Grissom as "a quiet little fellow who scoffs at the chance of becoming a hero". Here they are portrayed as regular guys; however, within a year of the publication of this feature all three underwent the extraordinary experience of being blasted into space.

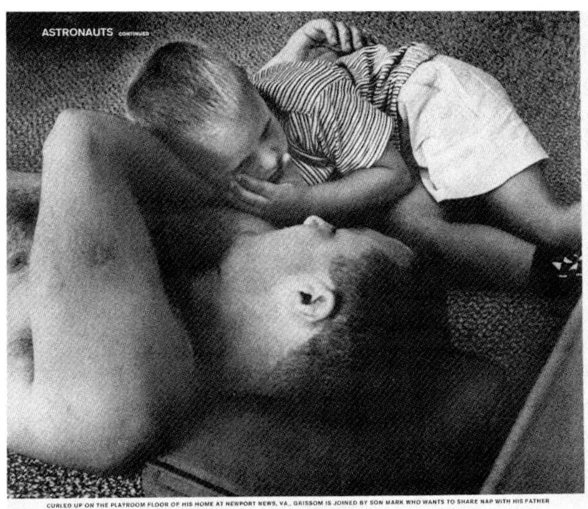

CURLED UP ON THE PLAYROOM FLOOR OF HIS HOME AT NEWPORT NEWS, VA., GRISSOM IS JOINED BY SON MARK WHO WANTS TO SHARE NAP WITH HIS FATHER

GRISSOM A QUIET LITTLE FELLOW WHO SCOFFS AT THE CHANCE OF BECOMING A HERO

Virgil ("Gus") Grissom, Captain, USAF, is, at 35, the youngest member of the three-man launch team. With his crew cut, short stature and earnest face he looks like TV's George Gobel. If any man with his experience in combat and test flying can be said to seem retiring, Grissom is that man. He is the easiest of the Astronauts to overlook, a pleasant little fellow who doesn't appear to have much get-up-and-go. To the casual observer he seems to be somewhat lost in the shadow of his larger and more outspoken colleagues.

But, as is true of John Glenn, Grissom's outward appearance is deceptive. His silence is not the result of the politeness he learned as a Boy Scout back home in Mitchell, Ind., nor is he a shy man. Grissom is simply not interested in making himself noticed and he refuses to take himself too seriously. He doesn't talk unless he has something to say and his comments are always exactly to the point. In a group at Cape Canaveral a few weeks ago the discussion turned to the Texas Tower disaster in which 28 had drowned when the structure fell into the sea. Someone in the group remarked that the Air Force would probably have trouble getting men to work on the other towers. Grissom looked at the speaker and smiled. "All they got to do," he said, "is cut the orders."

A big difference

Asked on another occasion about the difference between the Astronauts and other historic pioneers, he scoffed. "There's a big difference between us and Columbus and Lindbergh and the Wright brothers and all these people we're compared to. They did it themselves. We didn't think up this thing. We're just going to ride the capsule."

When he speaks of riding the capsule, Grissom is not underplaying the importance of the mission or of the pilot who makes it. His absorption with his job is complete. "This is the best thing that's ever happened to me," he says. "By the time I got into test work, it was dying out. It wasn't really flight test at all; it was mostly testing new gadgets. Here's a big new project with nothing but future. It's the first step in a great program that will go on as long as there are people."

What Grissom does repeatedly underplay is the importance of his personal role in the project and the fame that making one of the first flights might bring him: "Most people who know me know I'm not the hero type. Personal prestige I couldn't care less about. Sure, I want to make a success out of my military career, and this won't hurt that. But the notoriety the first man gets will only last for a little while and in a year or two the excitement of this will be forgotten in bigger things." Grissom does, however, have a solid confidence in his own capabilities, a confidence developed during 100 combat missions in Korea and in "gadget" testing for the Air Force when, on at least one occasion, he reports "a lot of people thought the mission was downright suicidal."

"I've always been reasonably competent," Grissom says, "and whenever I've started out with something new, I've been concerned that I won't perform like the big boys. I'm always surprised to find I can do as well as anybody else. I know I'm going to be scared when I get in there, but I don't worry about my feelings, and I'm not worried about being scared. I won't be scared very long. I know it's going to work."

Not enough time for home

Unlike Glenn, Gus Grissom does not believe in sharing his work experiences with his family. "Betty is interested in me," he says of his wife, "and if I have to do any homework, I try to wait until the kids go to bed. All the traveling hasn't helped the family any. I don't get time enough to see the boys and I don't think it's good for them. The older one, Scotty, is so interested in reading about space travel that it's hard to get him to read some of the other things he should be trying."

When they are all together, the Grissoms live simply, like the country folks they are. They are neither partygoers nor party-throwers. "Betty and I run our lives as we please," Grissom explains. "We don't care anything about fads or frills or the P.T.A. We don't give a damn about the Joneses."

A little bear of a man, Grissom does not hold himself to any particular conditioning routine, like Glenn's two-mile runs. He does keep his hands strong by squeezing a spring device and he is an excellent handball player. The only Astronaut ever to beat him at this game is Al Shepard, the third member of the launch team, and other Astronauts suggest that Grissom let Shepard win one game just because he wanted to so badly.

That would not be like Gus Grissom. He is a stubborn competitor and Shepard is another Astronaut. Each member of this unique group, in spite of any genuine camaraderie or solidarity, is interested in winning for himself. This interest applies particularly to the first flights. Asked a question about the strength of his desire for this, Grissom said, "Everything I do is influenced by it. With everything I do, I expect it. I'm here to ride the capsule."

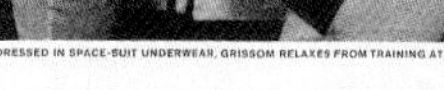

DRESSED IN SPACE-SUIT UNDERWEAR, GRISSOM RELAXES FROM TRAINING AT LANGLEY AIR FORCE BASE

HOUSEHOLD CHORE engages Grissom who fixes leaky roof of his house after a heavy snow. He lives in own home 17 miles from NASA center at Langley.

BIG PUSH by Grissom sends his sons Scott and Mark into pond behind the Grissom home. Grissom built the boat himself from plans in a magazine.

SUNDAY SPIN takes Grissom and wife Betty out on family bicycles. Grissom rides on bike which belongs to his oldest son, Scott. Betty rides her own.

PRIZED ENGINE in his *Corvette* is fussed over by Shepard. He likes car so much that instead of flying he drives it 300 miles from home to Canaveral.

TAKING IT EASY, Shepard sits on porch steps at Virginia Beach home with his wife Louise, niece Alice Williams *(left)*, daughters Louise *(center)*, Laura.

CUTTING UP for photographer, Shepard mugs during press conference after announcement of the Redstone team. The other Astronauts, from left, are Gordon Cooper, Donald Slayton, John Glenn, Scott Carpenter, Walter Schirra. The seventh man, Grissom, was in Bermuda on missile-tracking duty.

SHEPARD A COOL CUSTOMER AND A HOT PILOT WITH AN EYE FOR THE BIG PICTURE

Alan B. Shepard Jr., Commander, USN, is a man with a high barrier of reserve. "You might think you'd get to know someone well after working closely with him for almost two years," another Astronaut said. "Well, it's not that way with Shepard. He's always holding something back." It is not that Shepard is unfriendly or withdrawn. On the contrary, he has an easy charm and speaks out with poise, authority and often humor. But he does not give confidences. Behind the apparent candor he is wary, a cool studier of the situation.

The tallest (5 feet, 11 inches) of the Astronauts, Shepard holds his wiry frame with a loose grace and dresses, even in sports clothes, with a crisp immaculateness that reflects his Naval Academy training. He is not handsome, but his boyishly molded face gives a direct impression of character. Dressed in his bright orange flight suit and prowling around the Astronauts' jet fighter checking it out before take-off, his movements are delicate and sure. Totally and somehow caressingly absorbed in the huge machine, he is very much its master.

A high rating

The Astronauts rate each other realistically and Shepard rates high with the hard critics of this intimate clan. "He is very bright," says one of a very bright group. "He is an excellent pilot," says another member of the unique club whose members think they are the best pilots in the world. In a group where there is no designated leader Shepard is acknowledged to have real qualities of leadership. "The Navy lost a good officer when Al came into the program," one said. "He takes the admiral's view of the fleet. He feeds all the little items into place and isn't confused by details. Once he sets himself to an argument, he's tough and firm and usually right." Once during a discussion his admiral's view became so firm that his listener interrupted with, "Al, you're just another Astronaut to me."

Shepard's tongue is quick and he is sometimes funny. At a press conference called after the announcement of the team, John Glenn made a passing and jocular reference to the similarity between Ham, the chimpanzee which successfully rode the capsule, and the humans who would ride it later. Shepard looked up quickly and grinned. "Well, you said it, John," he cracked. "So, scratch."

A good athlete, Shepard likes to play golf and water ski, but he is particularly fond of his white, high-powered Corvette sports car, which he has had fitted with racing tires. Except for traffic laws and the chance that Project Mercury officials might look askance at such recklessness, he would love dearly to drive it just as fast and hard as it would go. Though one would think the lithe Shepard felt no particular need to keep himself in condition for a possible flight, he observed Glenn's running for a while and then took it up himself.

Shepard's alert intelligence is particularly noticeable in a group. Talking on subjects that interest him—for example, almost anything having to do with the technical and engineering aspects of Project Mercury—he is animated and well informed. People remember him, and he has the flattering social sense to remember others and their special areas of interest.

In his motel room near Cape Canaveral, Alan Shepard recently talked a bit about himself and about the mission he now has a good chance to fly. "I never have been my own favorite subject," he said, "and I don't think I've found anything new about myself since I've been in this program. We were asked to volunteer, not to become heroes. As far as I'm concerned, doing this is just a function of maturity. If you don't use your experience, your past is wasted, you are betraying yourself."

He mentioned his wife Louise, their two daughters and the niece who lives with them. "All this hasn't affected the family too much. I don't bring home the day-to-day crises. It's hard to hide a blow-up on the pad, but life goes on normally. The kids exhibit their mother's calm, rational approach to the problem.

"Once in a while I begin to wonder how the hell I'm going to feel, but I don't dwell on it. It's fine to think it's going to be a thrill, but it's more important to know what to do with all the knobs and the levers. Fear or distress comes from the unknown. The training in this program has helped us to know. It's a matter of confidence. I don't know just where the confidence begins, but it's there."

Shepard catches breath after a hard run, training for rigorous days ahead

Right: Dr. Wernher von Braun meeting Walt Disney in 1954. In the 1950s, von Braun worked with the Disney Studios as a technical director on a series of films about space exploration for American television.

one night spontaneously climbed on stage to join Bill Dana at the Cocoa Beach nightclub, Florida. Shepard knew the Jimenez routine by heart, and used excerpts in his radio communications to Gus Grissom on his Liberty Bell 7 flight on July 21, 1961. Just eight seconds into the flight Shepard joked, "Jose, don't cry too much", to which Grissom replied with the famous Jimenez line, "Oke-doke".

Jose Jimenez may have seemed like an innocent piece of fun to TV viewers in the early 1960s, but the character does highlight the point that at the time it was considered too ridiculous to even consider sending a non-white American into space. The theater of America's early space program was largely staged to appeal to the mainstream, white suburban audience, not the inner-city ghettos and deprived rural communities. As parts of the USA in the 1960s still segregated people on the basis of race, the space age did not belong to everybody.

Almost a year after the seven Mercury astronauts were presented to the world, the Chief Designer chose his first six cosmonauts: Valery Bykovsky, Gherman Titov, Grigory Nelmbov, Andrian Nikolayev, Pavel Popovich, and Yuri Gagarin. Like their American counterparts, all were young, super-fit pilots recommended by their military superiors; unlike their American counterparts, the team was not subjected to the scrutiny of the world's press.

The selection procedure was equally brutal for hopefuls on both sides. The short-listed candidates were stretched to the limits of human capability, probed, prodded and shaken, before the final decision was made. Such punishing tests would continue throughout the careers of both cosmonauts and astronauts.

Terms such as "astronaut", "cosmonaut", and "sputnik" represented the new vernacular of the space age and soon filtered into the popular vocabulary. They were new words for a new age and many other examples would follow. Words such as "countdown", "blastoff", and "A-OK" joined them when television and radio carried live coverage of rockets firing into space into people's homes. The first citizens of the space age now had a vocabulary to match the technological achievements of the day.

Newly elected President John F. Kennedy was quick to capitalize on the American public's growing

Top: Bill Dana as his comic creation Jose Jiminez, the reluctant astronaut. He appears here on the cover of a live recording of his famous routine, released through Kapp Records, Inc. in 1961.

The Evening News & The Star

World's largest evening sale

LONDON, WEDNESDAY, APRIL 12, 1961

LATE EDITION

PRICE 3d.

Back On Earth . . Major Yuri Gagarin Says: I Feel Well—No Injuries

MAN IN SPACE

Round World —And Back Alive!

MOSCOW, Wednesday.

RUSSIA has triumphed in the race to put man into space. She fired the first "Cosmonaut" into orbit to-day. He circled the earth every 89 minutes

OF MICE (And Dogs And Rabbits) AND MEN

Nov 1957 Laika, RUSSIA

July 1959 Snowflake & Daring, RUSSIAN

Nov 1957 Damka, RUSSIA

Belka, RUSSIA Aug 1960

May 1959

FOR NEWS FLE 6000
SMALL-ADS FLE 5000

TUG IN DOCK PERIL

WIFE KILLED

Top: A postage stamp commemorating a Soviet satellite launch in 1960. Postage stamps were often used to spread the word of space exploration.

Left: Soviet graphic designers often employed in their artwork a swooping line that mirrored the steep trajectory of a space-bound rocket.

Opposite and top right: The sleeves of two vinyl documentary recordings released in celebration of Gagarin's momentous trip.

Opposite top left: A British newspaper announces Yuri Gagarin's historic voyage into space with the story of several of the animals that preceded him; including the dogs, Laika and Belka.

appetite for outer space. He also soon realized the propaganda value of winning the battle in space, especially after the events of his fourth month in office. On April 8, 1961, the USSR unveiled Yuri Gagarin as the first cosmonaut they intended to shoot into space. Four days later the Supreme Soviet announced that he was in orbit around the Earth with the words: "A great event has taken place. For the first time in history man has accomplished a flight into space." The message continued with grand proclamations concerning the "powerful force of socialism" but ended with a call for peace and universal disarmament.

Gagarin was thrust into orbit inside the Vostok 1 spacecraft on April 12, 1961. The actual capsule, once in orbit and separated from its launch vehicle, was shaped like a fly. The spherical descent module was the only part of the craft that would return to Earth with Gagarin. Even so, the ball-like capsule was too heavy for a soft landing with the cosmonaut inside. It was equipped with an ejector seat, which enabled Gagarin to complete the last stage of his intrepid journey by parachute while the capsule thumped into the ground.

According to Reuters, "All Russia went wild with joy over the epoch-making voyage of the man whom Moscow Radio called the Columbus of the Interplanetary Age." The news was less well received in the USA where the Washington correspondent of the *Times* reported that, "Resigned disappointment and admiration were the main reactions". There were a few grumbles that the Soviets had kept the launch secret until Gagarin was actually in space—there were even rumors that he was safely back on earth by the time the announcement was made. Nevertheless, the newspapers were full of acclaim for Gagarin's daring exploit. A NASA press officer, who was awakened by a journalist, delivered a more down-to-earth reaction to the news, "It's three a.m. in the morning, you jerk", he yelled, "If you're wanting something from us, the answer is we are all asleep".

Congress was angry. Members wanted to know how and why the Russians had managed to humiliate the United States once again. One congressman suggested that if the American astronauts were too scared to fly into space he would offer himself as a volunteer for the first trip. Others were quick to point out the military implications of this act and also its effect on countries yet to decide between the capitalist and socialist systems. The media was also full of reports that there was no way the Americans could keep up with the Soviet achievements in space. America was considered the most powerful nation on earth and the Soviet Union was making a mockery of it. Since the early 1950s, the American public had read about the age of space travel and they eagerly awaited its arrival. Space was America's destiny, but

Left: Crowds in Moscow's Red Square celebrate the return of Russia's second man in space, cosmonaut Gherman Titov, on August 9, 1961. Titov flew in Vostok 2 on August 6, 1961.

Right: President John F. Kennedy, the man who made winning the space race a top priority for the USA, is driven through a welcome home parade in Cocoa Beach, Florida, with the superstar spaceman, John Glenn.

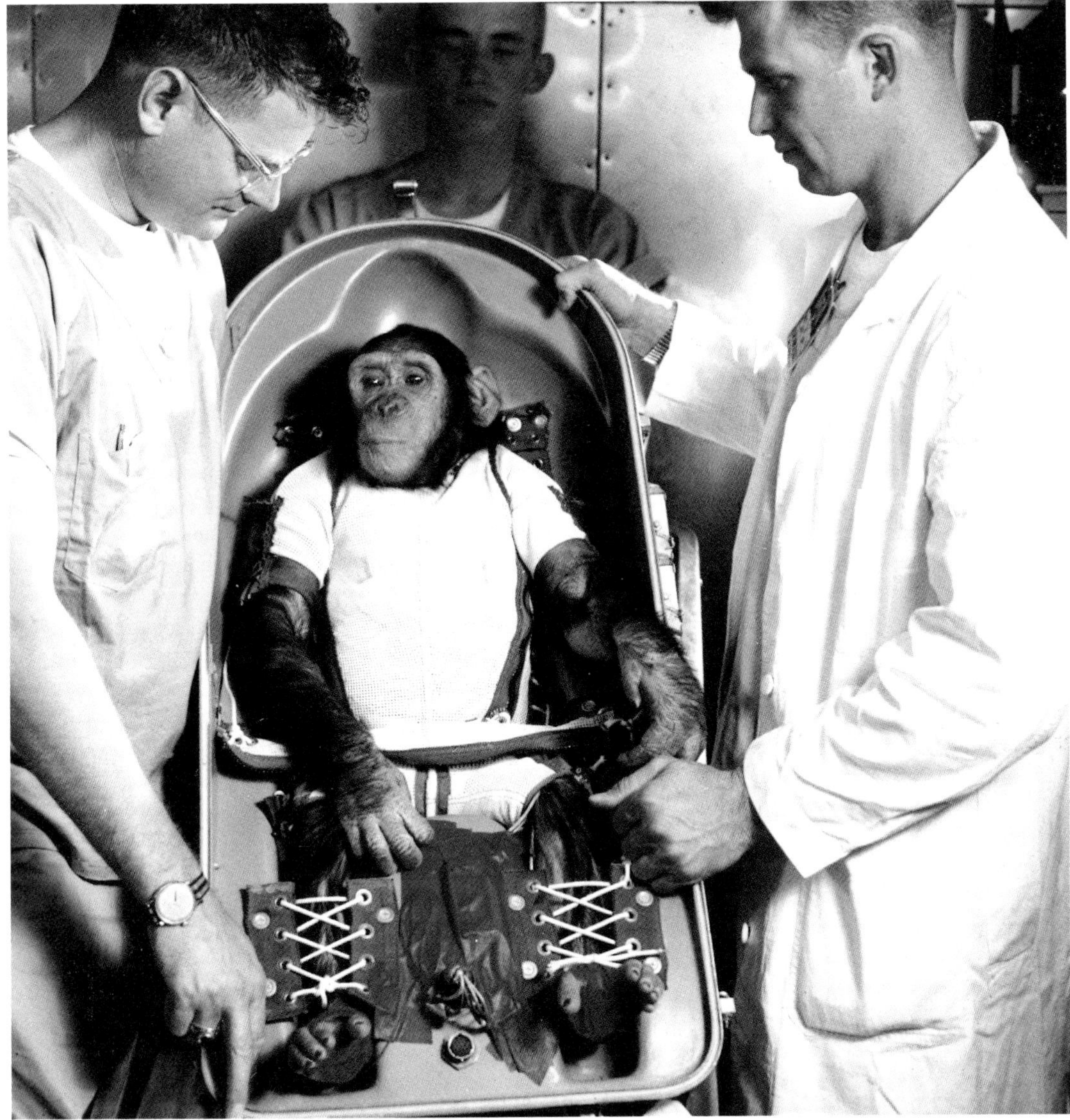

their dream of being the first to get there had now been shattered.

The Soviet government abandoned its usual endorsement of collective achievement and heaped adoration upon its first man in space. Reuters recorded the scene of Gagarin's return to Moscow in April 1961 as "the wildest public enthusiasm seen here since the end of the Second World War." In the following months Gagarin embarked on a world tour and his achievement was exploited to the full as propaganda for the Soviet system. Painters and sculptors across the USSR created heroic portraits and public monuments idolizing the handsome cosmonaut. His words from outer space were packaged and sold as vinyl recordings to commemorate the event. The recordings of his legendary words enabled people everywhere to own a piece of history and other souvenirs soon followed. The Soviet mail service issued a distinctive postage stamp on the day of the launch to celebrate the achievement, a tradition that

Left: NASA also sent animals into space to monitor the effects before risking human lives. Ham, a three-year-old chimpanzee, is pictured here in the biopack couch used aboard his Mercury-Redstone suborbital test flight on January 31, 1961.

Right: Astronaut John Glenn climbing into the Mercury-Atlas capsule Friendship 7 prior to the first American manned Earth orbital mission.

was repeated many times over on subsequent launches in both the USSR and the USA.

One of the most ironic aspects of Gagarin's achievement was that it sprang from a country where freedom of movement was heavily restricted. Most Soviet citizens were not able to move freely within the borders of their own country but now they celebrated because one of their comrades had orbited the earth. However, the flight of Vostok 1 was controlled from the ground, the first cosmonaut was a passenger rather than a pilot, and there was no way that Gagarin, even if he had so wished, could have used the flight to defect from Russia. He may have circled the globe but he would never be able to leave the grip of his Soviet masters.

Gagarin's reports from his pioneering trip provide an invaluable, first-hand account of the experience of being in outer space. Nowadays, photographs of the earth taken from beyond its atmosphere are commonplace, but in 1961 nobody had ever seen such images. Gagarin's descriptions were the first that anybody had brought back from space. The simple description of what he saw and felt brought human emotions to the space age, primed the audience on the ground, and left them eager for more. He was sent into space to take a look around on behalf of everybody on Earth and this is what he reported: "During the flight I saw for the first time with my own eyes the Earth's spherical shape. You can see its curvature when looking to the horizon. I must say that the view of the horizon is unique and very beautiful." Gagarin also described the point at which the Earth's atmosphere ends and outer space begins: "It is possible to see the remarkably colorful change from the light surface of the Earth to the completely black sky in which one can see the stars. This dividing line is very thin, just like a belt of film surrounding the Earth's sphere. It is of a delicate blue color. And this transition from the blue to the dark is very gradual and lovely. When I emerged from the shadow of the Earth, the horizon looked different. There was a bright orange strip along it, which again passed into a blue hue and once again into a dense black color." He then spoke of outer space and the stars: "I did not see the moon. In space the sun is shining tens of times brighter than on Earth. Stars are very well seen. They are bright and distinct. The whole picture of the sky is more contrasted than when it is seen from the Earth."

Another part of Gagarin's task was to report the physical sensation of being weightless in outer space: "Everything was easier to perform.... legs and arms weighed nothing.... Objects are swimming in the cabin, and myself, I did not sit in the chair, as before, but I was suspended in mid-air. During the state of weightlessness I ate and drank, and everything was like on Earth." Recounting these experiences for the first time, Gagarin provided images and sensations that would inspire artists and designers for decades to come.

In the meantime, NASA still had to launch the first American into space. America's national pride had once again taken a battering. The world was laughing at the USA and Kennedy had to find a way to stop it. He sent a memo to Vice President Lyndon B. Johnson and numerous space experts asking for advice on what could be done.

Around 45 million Americans tuned in their TV sets to watch Alan B. Shepard lift off from Cape Canaveral in the Mercury capsule he had

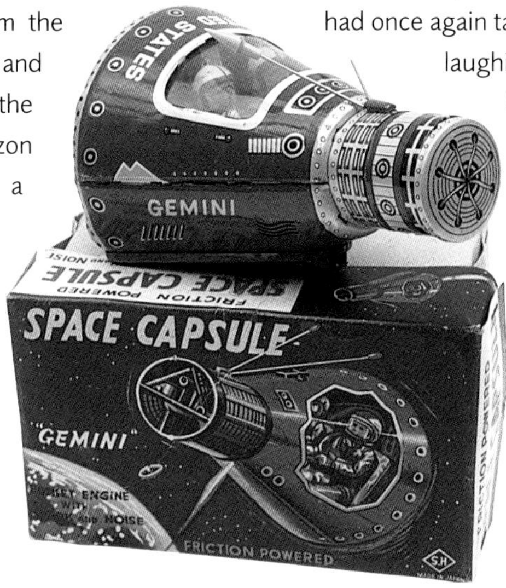

Left: Space-age toys gradually became more life-like as the fantasy of space travel was overtaken by the real thing. This Gemini capsule toy of c. 1965 is a replica of the real spacecraft.

christened Freedom 7. As he left the ground, his colleague Donald "Deke" Slayton, mimicking the Jose Jimenez character, radioed: "You're on your way, Jose." This Mercury 3 mission was not an orbital space flight. Shepard was fired up into space and then fell back to Earth, as the Redstone rocket was not powerful enough to put him into orbit.

Live TV coverage put extra pressure on NASA to succeed with this flight. It meant that viewers at home could share in the unfolding drama and if anything had gone wrong, it would have happened with millions watching. It only lasted fifteen minutes, but the flight went as planned. After splashdown in the Atlantic Ocean, Shepard's Mercury 3 capsule was lifted by helicopter aboard the aircraft carrier, Lake Champlain. He let himself out of the capsule and exclaimed, "Boy, what a ride" before introducing himself to the ship's crew with the phrase, "My name Jose Jimenez." The launch and mission was a complete success and the nation celebrated. It was just the tonic America needed. On his return, Shephard was given a hero's welcome with a jubilant parade through Washington DC and a lavish White House reception.

Amid the celebrations, Kennedy's advisors were busy formulating America's giant step into space. Kennedy took their thoughts into consideration and on May 25, 1961, he spoke to Congress, declaring: "I believe this nation should commit itself to achieving the goal, before this decade is out, of landing a man on the moon and returning him safely to Earth." Commenting on the new goal, Wernher von Braun noted its simplicity and understandable nature: "Everybody knows what the moon is, everybody knows what this decade is, and everybody can tell a live astronaut who returned from the moon from one who didn't." However, a number of skeptics and conspiracy theorists would later disagree with that final assumption.

Whatever Khrushchev and the Supreme Soviet had intended with the Chief Designer's victories in space, there can be no doubting the massive repercussions they had in the United States. The USSR had succeeded in landing a succession of devastating blows to the self-esteem of their superpower rival. In so doing, the Soviets also devised a makeover for themselves and transformed their international image from a backwards dictatorship into a formidable industrial powerhouse. Now, with President Kennedy's declaration, the Soviet Union had succeeded in influencing American policy to such an extent that the United States had committed itself to spending many billions of dollars—depleting their resources elsewhere—on a race to the moon that was essentially against the clock.

There were many more obstacles to overcome before either a Soviet or an American would set foot on the moon: a manned lunar voyage was an entirely

Opposite: Manufacturers promoted the space-age attributes of numerous time-saving convenience foods. One of the more memorable campaigns was for Cadbury's Smash brand of instant mashed potato (c. 1970) which featured a band of space-exploring robots.

different proposition to a simple orbit around the Earth. But after each mission—Mercury, Gemini, and Apollo in the USA and Vostok, Voskhod, and Soyuz in the USSR—the minds behind the respective space programs discovered more and more about how this goal might one day be accomplished.

Virgil "Gus" Grissom became the second American astronaut to make the journey into space, but like Shepard's trip, Mercury 4 was a suborbital mission. The Chief Designer launched Vostok 2 on August 6, 1961, and pitched Gherman Titov into space for a total of seventeen orbits around the Earth. On his return he became the first cosmonaut to visit the United States. The host for his visit and the first American to go into orbit was the superstar spaceman, John Glenn.

Kennedy rallied the nation behind his mission to reach the moon. The speech he gave placed greater emphasis than ever before on the necessity for America to win the battle in space. National pride now depended on results in outer space and there would be no respite until America won. The president gave space explor-ation even greater significance and public interest swelled enormously by the time astronaut John Glenn took his trip into outer space. A few hundred onlookers gathered on the beaches near Cape Canaveral to witness the failed launch of the Vanguard rocket in 1957. When John Glenn took off in the Friendship 7 capsule in 1962 on top of the new Atlas rocket, estimates put the number of onlookers at fifty thousand. Gay Talese, writing in the New York Times described the scene shortly before the launch at Cocoa Beach, Florida: "Fifty thousand spectators stood along the beach watching the climbing Atlas carrying Lieut. Col. John H. Glenn Jr. into orbit. Some cheered and clapped. An elderly woman said solemnly: 'He's in the hands of the Lord now.' Most remained silent." Other accounts noted that the mood across the USA was "strangely calm" and "anxious" while Glenn was in space.

Right: Children were well aware of the excitement that accompanied the new era of space travel. This was capitalized upon by confectionery manufacturers in the late 1960s and early 1970s who incorporated space-age imagery into designs for all kinds of sweet wrappers.

Transistor radios kept people all over the world informed of the astronaut's progress. In New York, people "walked the streets like those afflicted with tooth-ache, transistor radios clapped against cheeks and ears." On Cocoa Beach, "radios in cars, on people's shoulders and in their pockets could be heard everywhere". Also, in New York, a TV screen nearly 4 x 5 meters in size was erected on the central mezzanine in Grand Central Station. As many as nine thousand commuters stood shoulder-to-shoulder to watch the launch of Glenn's Mercury 6 mission. The images that flickered across the giant screen were said to "magnify the drama" and the "involvement of the crowds."

John Glenn embodied all the attributes of a typical white American hero. He was a clean-cut, fair-haired, wholesome family man, and to top it all, a regular churchgoer and Sunday-school teacher. His star quality had been apparent at the very first press conference the astronauts gave and now the nation waited nervously for him to return safely from outer space. However, the mission did not proceed as planned.

The flight control team on Earth first became concerned when an illuminated signal indicated that the spacecraft's heat shield had separated prematurely from the capsule. If this was indeed the case then the astronaut would be burned alive when he reentered the Earth's atmosphere. NASA had a real life cliffhanger on its hands; just like in a movie, their hero was enduring a

perilous climax before the resolution of his adventure. A few more checks suggested that the signal was probably faulty rather than the equipment, but this was not a certainty. Radio contact was not possible during reentry and Glenn's family, fellow astronauts, and spectators around the world waited a nail-biting four minutes and twenty seconds to hear his fate.

Down on Earth, television showrooms were jammed with onlookers waiting nervously for any news. Alan B. Shepard at ground control repeatedly tried to radio the capsule and asked, "Friendship 7, this is Cape, do you read?" Finally the reply came, "Loud and clear." Glenn was alive but it had been an uncertain return to Earth.

Celebrations erupted immediately in Manhattan, where there was a spontaneous storm of tickertape and scenes of impromptu celebration not witnessed since the end of World War II. Down on Cocoa Beach, a huge cake, the size and shape of Glenn's Mercury capsule, was sliced and shared among the revellers. According to Gay Talese, the resort's "jazz bands and cash registers were swinging and ringing in merry syncopation."

The John Glenn phenomenon is perhaps the foremost example of the way space exploration fired the public's imagination. The following day's newspapers were saturated with advertisements for products as diverse as computers and coffee, all celebrating John Glenn's feat. Food, especially sweet food, became a very popular means of celebrating space travel as its impact reached into unexpected markets. Where the Russians had smoked their way into the space age with Laika cigarettes, kids in the West could eat their way into it. Sweet cigarettes such as Space Patrol enabled children to mimic adults' smoking habits with confectionery. Mouth-popping Spacedust was another favorite, along with rocket-shaped frozen lollies with names like Zoom, Sky Ray, and Blastoff.

Left: Not only was the space age colorful and exciting, it tasted good too.

Glenn's Friendship 7 capsule embarked on a world tour and visited over fifteen different countries in a display of America's technological prestige. Space enthusiasts were able to witness, close-up, an actual spacecraft—not a movie prop, but a real, bona fide spaceship. The capsule returned to the USA later that year and made an appearance at the 1962 Seattle World's Fair, where the newly built Space Needle had been unveiled. This sixty-story tower points dramatically toward the stars and stands as a monument to the optimism of the space age. At its summit is a revolving restaurant, which orbits the central tower and mirrors the flight path of a satellite.

The mood after John Glenn's trip was optimistic. There was a popular feeling that if human beings could travel into space then surely anything was possible. When the people cheered they were not only expressing relief at the astronaut's safe return, they were celebrating their new-found faith in the future. Everything was going to be all right. Glenn, however, was not to make any further trips into space and he retired from service in 1964. Rumor has it that John F. Kennedy personally gave instructions that John Glenn was not to be risked on any future missions into space. Kennedy believed that the astronaut was a national treasure and far too valuable to the country to be sent out on further, dangerous missions.

August 1962 and June 1963 saw the Soviet Union perform yet more stunts in space with the last four of the Vostok flights. Vostok 3 and Vostok 4 were launched in sequence less than a day apart. The two spacecraft performed an approximate rendezvous and came within 5 km of each other's orbit. Andrian Nikolayev in Vostok 3 became the first person to make a live TV broadcast from space, and his wife-to-be, Valentina Tereshkova, hit the headlines the following year by becoming the first woman in space.

Radio had been the main source of information at the start of the space age. Listeners had been able to hear actual sounds transmitted live from outer space by satellites since the launch of Sputnik 1. The Soviet Union made full use of short-wave radio to ensure people everywhere knew Sputnik 1 had made it into space. Radio broadcasts continued to play a big part in all missions and engaged listeners while they went about their daily routine. However, the role of television expanded rapidly as it proved to be an effective weapon in the propaganda battle for space supremacy. It was no longer considered enough to bring back words—the people wanted pictures.

NASA carried its manned launches live on television, but the Soviet authorities were much more secretive and deprived its citizens of sharing in the tension of a countdown. Viewers in the USA watched astronauts prepare for launch as nervously as if they themselves were about to be shot into space. The coverage ended on earlier missions as the rocket climbed out of view. People on Earth could only imagine the amazing sights beyond the stratosphere

Top: The 1962 hit single *Telstar* by The Tornados, an instrumental pop group that attempted to capture the excitement of the new era in music.

Opposite: Moscow. Lessons at a radio study group, receiving satellite signals from Sputnik.

Top: A TV camera is very prominent in this illustration from a 1967 Soviet postage stamp, an indication of the growing contribution television was making to the propaganda war in space.

that the cosmonauts and astronauts were witnessing first hand. When Gagarin flew around the Earth he had sent back words; Nikolayev in Vostok 3 sent back pictures—moving pictures. His trip set the standard for future missions in space and the TV camera became an essential piece of kit. "TV cameras", as journalist Jack Gould commented, "made it possible for the world to see what astronauts, both American and Russian, have had such difficulty in reducing to words." Television took viewers to the center of the action. It provided an emotional tether between the astronauts and the people watching at home.

Space travel also revolutionized the way in which television signals were transmitted. The Telstar satellite reached orbit in July 1962 and was used to transmit the first transatlantic television broadcast. The achievement was later celebrated in the hit single *Telstar* by pop group The Tornados. Communications technology was transformed by the ability of satellites to bounce and amplify signals to and from the Earth. The space age spanned the demise of the industrial era and heralded the start of a new age of information. Satellites speed up the rate at which information can be exchanged and represent the most substantial commercial use of outer space.

The two years following the final Vostok and Mercury missions saw very little action in terms of manned flights into space. There was not another American manned space flight until March 1965. Events were just as quiet in the USSR and the first Voskhod flight did not fly until October 1964. Events back on Earth were much more volatile. Kennedy, the optimist who had instigated America's excursion to the moon, was assassinated in November, 1963. His successor, Lyndon B. Johnson, had been instrumental in formulating the planned lunar landing but the escalating war in Vietnam rather than the space race dominated his term in office. In the USSR, Khrushchev was deposed as the Soviet leader in 1964 and the Chief Designer was terminally ill.

Project Gemini was introduced as a stepping-stone project between the early Mercury missions and the gigantic Apollo program. It was certainly a turning point in the battle over outer space. The massive amount of state funding being channelled into NASA was taking effect. Bigger launch sites, a new control center, and numerous research facilities were appearing across America with a concentration in the Southern states. The USA was now launching many more successful vessels into space than the USSR. Many newspapers still claimed that the USSR was ahead in the space race, but the massive investment in NASA now dwarfed that of the Soviet space program. America was spending its way to the moon. A primary objective of the Gemini missions was to enable astronauts to leave their capsule and take a walk in outer space. The Soviets, however, stole the headlines yet again.

Left: On June 3, 1965 Edward H. White II became the second person to take a walk in space. In his right hand White carries a Hand-Held Self Maneuvering Unit which he used to move about in the weightless environment of space. The gold plating on his visor protected his eyes from the unfiltered rays of the sun. The astronaut remained attached to his Gemini 4 capsule by a long umbilical cord, which adds to the impression in this photograph of a fetus floating inside a womb.

On March 18, 1965, Lieutenant Colonel Alexei Leonov left his capsule, Voskhod 2, to become the first person to walk freely in space. Millions of TV viewers across Europe and the USSR watched blurry pictures of Colonel Leonov emerge from his capsule and push himself into the darkness. Leonov spent a total of twenty minutes outside his cabin at the end of a 4.6-meter-long lifeline. Three months later, on June 3, 1965, American astronaut Edward White performed a similar feat. He was so excited by the experience that ground control had to order White repeatedly to return to the capsule. White's space walk was captured in some magnificent color photographs that show him hovering upside-down over the curvature of the Earth. The photographs taken in space provided an endless source of fascination on Earth. Images of astronauts and spacecraft were used in packaging by all kinds of manufacturers as a means of showing they were with the times.

The Gemini project provided the opportunity for the original seven astronauts to practice all kinds of different maneuvers and share their expertise with a

band of new recruits. In the subsequent Gemini missions the team practised docking procedures with other craft and endured ever lengthier stays in space. Everything was methodically rehearsed before any mission went live and contingency plans were developed to cover any imaginable emergency. Every assignment was a valuable learning experience for all the astronauts and ground crew involved in preparation for Apollo.

The second space walk by an American took place on the Gemini 9 voyage, which became known as the mission of the "Angry Alligator." The Gemini 9 capsule was scheduled to link up with an automated spacecraft used to practice docking. However, when the crew came across their target vessel its protective nose cone had not been jettisoned. Instead, its clam-shell-like casing became jammed and resembled the open jaws of an alligator.

Project Gemini saw NASA undertake ten manned missions within a time span of eighteen months from March 1965 to November 1966. It was a period of intense activity in space for the Americans and there was plenty of optimism about what they might achieve. There was talk of establishing colonies on the moon and trips to Mars. The technology that fuelled the excursions into space was going to solve the major

Top: The jammed nose cone of the "Angry Alligator", Gemini 9's Augmented Target Docking Adapter, June 3, 1966.

Left: Vehicle for Lunar Landing Research Facility at Langley Research Center, Hampton, Virginia, USA, May 1963.

Right: The Apollo 7 Saturn IB space vehicle is launched from the Kennedy Space Center's Launch Complex 34 on October 11, 1968. A tracking antenna is seen in the foreground on the left.

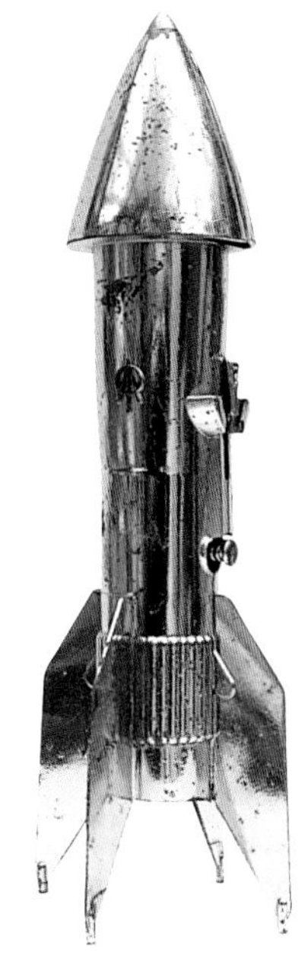

problems on Earth. New synthetic materials helped reduce production costs of everyday products and promised a revolution in the home. The doubt and hesitation expressed at the first Soviet victories was on the decline; the future looked bright.

The USSR managed only two manned missions during the time span of Project Gemini. Although Voskhod 1 was the first spacecraft to carry three people into space, it was apparent that the Soviet Union was falling behind the United States. On January 14, 1966, the Chief Designer, the anonymous figure who had driven the Soviet space program since its inception, died on the operating table at the age of 59. The Chief Designer was given a full state funeral and was afforded the highest honor of having his ashes interred in the Kremlin Wall. The Soviet press mourned his passing with obituaries detailing his exceptional career and his true identity. His name: Sergei Korolev.

A full rehearsal for the launch of the first Apollo flight took place on January 27, 1967. The countdown was fraught with difficulties, particularly in regard to communications. A small fire started in the cockpit. The capsule's pressurized atmosphere of pure oxygen meant that it took only a few seconds for the flames to engulf the entire cabin. The spacecraft was packed with flammable materials, which fed the fire and released toxic smoke. Escape hatches proved impossible to open and by the time a rescue team arrived it was too late. The three astronauts, Roger B. Chaffee, Edward White, and Virgil "Gus" Grissom, were burned alive. Project Apollo was suspended for almost two years while investigations into the fire took place.

Top: Three toy rockets. The Apollo X Moon Challenger (c. 1969) on the left closely resembles the Apollo 7 Saturn IB rocket shown on the opposite page. The money-box in the center was made in Detroit in 1957. The friction toy on the right was produced in Eastern Europe in the 1960s.

Meanwhile, the Soviets had a new Chief Designer. His name was Vasili Mishin and although he had been a deputy and colleague of Korolev since 1945, he lacked his predecessor's power and influence in political circles. Without Korolev's authority, the Soviet space program lost its cohesion. Bitter infighting and power struggles between the many different departments and directors took its toll on Soviet efforts in space. It was not long after the Apollo tragedy that the new Chief Designer had a catastrophe of his own to deal with. The first Soyuz mission left its launch pad just three months after the fire in the first Apollo. The launch was fine but trouble hit as soon as the spacecraft reached orbit. Soyuz 1, piloted by Vladimir Komarov, was due to link up with Soyuz 2 but a number of technical faults meant the plan had to be abandoned. Komarov prepared to return Soyuz 1 to Earth. The parachutes that should have slowed down the capsule on its descent became entangled and failed to open. The tumbling spacecraft hit the ground with such an impact that the cosmonaut was killed.

Yuri Gagarin was back-up to Komarov and scheduled to fly in Soyuz 3, his first mission since Vostok 1. During a training flight in March 1968, he flew a two-seater jet fighter through another aircraft's slipstream. The turbulence sent Gagarin's jet out of control. The first human being to see the Earth from outer space was dead. Gagarin, like Sergei Korolev, was honored by having his ashes entombed in the Kremlin Wall. The first Soviet space station, Salyut, was named as a salute to Gagarin's heroic achievement.

The space age had claimed its first victims, and the losses hung over all those involved in space exploration. The initial excitement that had characterized the Gemini and Vostok missions was replaced with questions over the human cost of this quest to reach the moon. The break in the Apollo schedule gave people time to consider what the conquest of space actually meant. Later rocket launches still pulled in the viewers but opposition to the Apollo missions grew louder.

The enthusiasm that accompanied the Mercury and Gemini flights became tempered with a mood of ambivalence. A doctor, quoted in an article by Sandra Blakeslee of the *New York Times*, echoed the uncertainty of the American public toward Project Apollo: "I'm confused about the space program. I'm happy when we meet with success but I keep wondering if we should be doing this when we have so many problems." The confusion, suggested Blakeslee, arose because people felt "catapulted into an alien age that they do not understand." Progress was happening too quickly. "What was once science fiction," stated the journalist, "is turning dizzily into scientific fact and for some, it is hard to keep pace." Blakeslee concluded that this fear of the future was contributing to the growing apathy toward space travel and suggested, "some adults, while verbally uncertain of their feelings toward the moon

Left: Taken by the crew of Apollo 8 on December 24, 1968, this picture represents the very first time human eyes witnessed the phenomenon known as Earthrise.

exploration are emotionally opposed if not outright afraid of it."

Almost two years after the tragic fire that killed their colleagues, the Apollo 7 crew of Walter Schirra, Don Eisele, and Walter Cunningham were launched into space by von Braun's enormous Saturn V rocket. Saturn V was awesome: at 110 meters high it was taller than the Statue of Liberty. The rocket's power was so immense that NASA officials at Cape Canaveral thought it prudent to move the press box over 5.6 km away from the launch pad. Even so, a commentator for CBS News was startled when the ceiling of his Cape Canaveral studio collapsed on top of him during a Saturn V test flight. The fire in the first Apollo resulted in the introduction of many new materials and safety measures into the new spacecraft. Intensive research was undertaken in the development of fire resistant foams, plastics, and other synthetic materials.

Apollo 8 was the first manned mission to leave Earth orbit and make the enormous journey to the moon. The crew consisted of Frank Borman, William Anders, and James Lovell. The three astronauts made several TV broadcasts during the trip and sent back to Earth some of the most profound images yet to be taken in space. The most memorable of the broadcasts came on Christmas Eve, 1968. Their words made the perfect accompaniment to their photographs, which contrast the barren surface of the moon with the distant, fertile Earth. Astronaut James Lovell captured a very special moment when he commented: "The vast loneliness up here is awe-inspiring, and it makes you realize just what you have back there on Earth. The Earth from here is a grand oasis in the big vastness of space." His words were a fitting gift to the viewers watching him from Earth—a realization of the value of their own planet. The photographs taken of the Earth from lunar orbit handed a potent symbol to the growing environmental movement. They showed the Earth as a luscious yet vulnerable object against an expanse of nothing.

The longer stays in space needed to reach the moon called for many innovations in the most basic aspects of life. The astronauts had to eat, exercise regularly, wash, and use the toilet. While the Mercury and Gemini missions had been akin to long-haul flights, the Apollo missions went on for days. Equipment had to be space-saving and as light as possible if it was to accompany the three astronauts in their Apollo capsule. Space explorers transformed their confined quarters between states for working, living, and sleeping, and similar notions of capsule living gained popularity back on Earth. Whereas nourishment for the astronauts came as processed food in sealed plastic bags, products that saved time or space around the home were marketed in ways that highlighted their space-age attributes. Manufacturers sold ranges of "instant" foodstuffs as the convenience cuisine of the space age. One of the most memorable campaigns came from Cadbury's, which used a band of colorful, space-

BELL'S SCOTCH WHISKY

London Monday June 7, 1971 No. 27,195 3p

Evening News

Night Special

Now Russia has a two-year lead over the Americans

RUSSIANS CHECK IN AT SPACE HOTEL

Hospital probes Labour MP's death

By PETER KANE

Dreadful pain

Coughing

JAGGER FINDS HIS HOME IN THE SUN

£10,000 BET WINNER GOES INTO HIDING

Cholera beats city cordon

From Reuter Correspondent IAN MacKENZIE

CALCUTTA

BRITAIN

MYSTERY OF £40,000 COINS 'RAID'

Evening News Reporter

Top: A newspaper headline announcing the arrival of three cosmonauts at Salyut 1, the first true space station, June 7, 1971.

Left: The first experimental space station, comprising of Soyuz 4 and Soyuz 5, pictured at the Cosmos Pavilion, Moscow, April 1970.

exploring robots to advertise its Smash brand of instant mashed potatoes.

The Soviets, without Korolev and only a fraction of the funding made available to NASA, struggled to maintain pace with the American missions into space. They continued to develop a lunar program with a series of unmanned circumlunar flights by Zond spacecraft in 1968, 1969, and 1970. Mishin was engaged in a struggle with a vital component in Korolev's legacy known as the N-1—a huge rocket to equal the size and power of Saturn V. The first test launch of the N-1 occurred in February 1969. It left the ground but a malfunction caused the shutdown of all its engines, and it fell back to Earth.

The second attempt came in July 1969, two weeks before the launch of Apollo 11. Again it left the ground but the N-1 became the biggest rocket to explode on its launch pad. The result was total devastation of the Soviet launch facility at Baikonur, Kazakhstan. It killed over 100 people and the complex took over two years to rebuild. Despite the N-1's failure (which remained a state secret for many years) the Soviets continued to send probes to the moon as if they were still in the race. However, American spy satellites had recorded the devastation at Baikonur and gave assurance to NASA that their men would be first on the moon. The N-1 catastrophe switched Soviet attention away from the moon to the establishment of Salyut, a manned Earth-orbiting space station.

Apollo missions 9 and 10 provided the opportunity to test the new lunar module's capabilities without actually touching down on the moon's surface. That important step belonged to Apollo 11.

An estimated one million people braved the hot Florida sunshine to witness the thunderous lift-off of Apollo 11 on its epic journey to the moon. The roads around Cape Canaveral were packed with cars in lines over 16 km long. The Apollo 11 launch took place on July 16, 1969, and three days later, the astronauts Neil Armstrong, Edwin "Buzz" Aldrin, and Michael Collins braked into lunar orbit. Collins remained in the Command Module, Columbia, while Armstrong and Aldrin flew the Lunar Module, Eagle, to the surface of the moon. Tension mounted as the on-board computer nearly brought them down in a crater of hazardous rocks, but relief came when Cape Canaveral heard the words: "Tranquillity Base here. The Eagle has landed." Neil Armstrong left the vessel some six hours after touchdown to become the first human to set foot on the moon. He was joined by Aldrin fifteen minutes later. They were watched by the largest television audience in history, but not all the viewers believed what they saw. Some thought it was an elaborate hoax and suggested that NASA filmed the whole event on a stage set to assert America's prestige without having to make the trip to the moon. Back in 1961, when Wernher von Braun had said "Everybody can tell a live astronaut who returned from the moon from one who didn't," he had failed to account for the conspiracy theorists who cried "fake."

Left: Astronaut Edwin E. Aldrin poses for a photograph on the lunar surface beside the raised flag of the United States. The picture was taken by Neil Armstrong, the first man to set foot on the moon.

On the moon Aldrin and Armstrong performed experiments, collected rock samples, raised a flag, unveiled a plaque, and endured a telephone call with President Nixon. It was all over in just over two-and-a-half hours. The intrepid pair, their outfits filthy with moon dust, returned to the Eagle and settled down for a night on the moon. The Eagle lifted off the next day, flattening the Stars and Stripes, and joined Columbia for the journey home. On their return, the three astronauts were sealed into a mobile quarantine facility and taken to the NASA complex at Houston where they remained for a further three weeks. Then came a 45-day world tour and a grueling schedule of engagements and ceremonies.

The moon landing ended centuries of speculation but provoked conflicting reactions among those who witnessed it. Some saw it as an abhorrent waste of resources, whereas others marveled at the awesome spectacle. Most agree that it was one of the greatest technological achievements in history, but many also questioned its purpose. The playwright Arthur Miller summed up the different opinions: "There are two schools of thought about the moon landing. One heralds it as the start of a new Age of Discovery like the period that began in 1492. The other regards it as a distraction from social problems." Race riots, civil unrest and opposition to the war in Vietnam raised pressing issues that were closer to home. Many thought that the money spent on reaching the moon would be put to better use solving problems on Earth.

However, the loud protests were nowhere near as damaging to the space program as the American government's spending cuts. The exorbitant cost of each mission was a huge drain on national resources. Budget restrictions in 1969 and 1970 caused three of the scheduled Apollo lunar landings to be scrapped. The flights proved too expensive and the Nixon administration needed extra funds to continue the war in Vietnam. The grand spectacle of the space race was fast drawing to a close.

Even so, Project Apollo still had plenty of fans. Apollo 12 left the Earth on November 14, 1969, but moments after clearing the launch tower the rocket was struck by lightning. The resulting power surge knocked out many vital systems. The crew of Charles "Pete" Conrad, Alan Bean, and Richard Gordon managed to rectify the situation and the mission continued on its voyage to the moon. Conrad and Bean spent a total of 31-and-a-half hours on the lunar surface and made two excursions to explore the new world and conduct more experiments. They made it home safely with 34 kg of moon rock and a few pieces of Surveyor 3, a robotic probe that had been on the moon since April 1967.

Apollo 13 became a legendary mission for all the wrong reasons. An explosion ripped the Service Module apart just as the spacecraft approached lunar orbit. The moon landing was cancelled and the crew of James Lovell, John Swigert, and Fred Haise, were lucky to make it back alive. The perilous voyage drew a huge television audience, but again

raised questions about the human cost of these epic journeys. The USSR took advantage of the lull after Apollo 13 to fire a remote-controlled probe to the moon in November 1970. The bizarre contraption, called Lunakhod 1, resembled a bath-tub on wheels. All manner of unusual devices were attached to it, including a huge heat-shielding disc and a ray-gun-like antenna. The lunar rover's mission was to return samples of lunar soil to the USSR and it achieved this, as the Soviet authorities readily pointed out, without risk to human life and at a fraction of the cost of the Apollo flights.

The USSR then focused its efforts on establishing Salyut 1, the first manned, Earth-orbiting space station. It was first visited on June 7, 1971, by the Soyuz 11 crew of Viktor Patsayev, Georgi Dobrovolsky, and Vladislav Volkov. The event was announced in the London *Evening News* under the headline: "Russians Check in at Space Hotel." Salyut renewed interest in the Soviet space

Top: Lunakhod 1, the Soviet Union's remote-controlled moon explorer vehicle. It was launched on November 10, 1970.

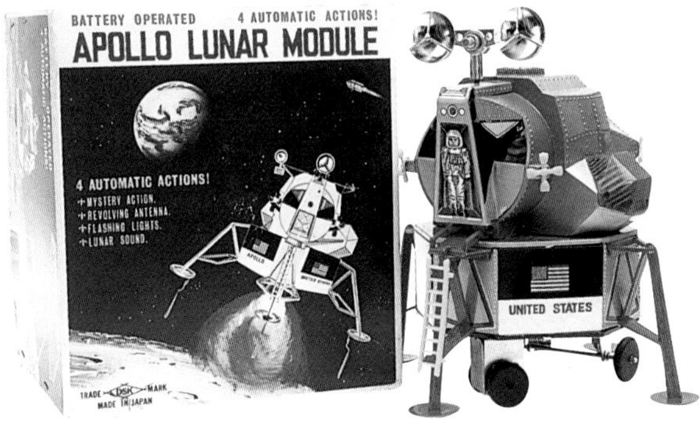

Left: Toy replica of the Apollo Lunar Module. Plastic grew in popularity during the 1960s and replaced tin as the material for toy makers, a move that was mirrored in the manufacture of homeware, furniture, and other domestic products.

agenda, but sadly, the three cosmonauts perished on their return to Earth on June 29, 1971. It was over two years before a manned Soviet mission flew again.

Project Apollo saw the end of space travel as a public spectacle. Increased cooperation in space exploration between the Soviet Union and the United States lessened its relevance as a tactic of the Cold War. The scientific exploration of space did not deliver the same instant satisfaction as the earlier ratings-boosting manned space flights. The days of the thrilling four-hour trip were gone. Space exploration was no longer a speedy white-knuckle ride, more a sleepy long-haul flight.

The Apollo 15 mission saw the first appearance of the moon buggy, a small car developed for driving on the lunar surface. It enabled astronauts to cover much greater distances than before and make the most of their limited time up there. Apollo 17 was the final lunar mission, leaving the Earth on December 7, 1972. Eugene Cernan, Ronald Evans, and Harrison Schmitt left a plaque with the following inscription: "Here man completed his first explorations of the moon, December 1972 AD. May the spirit of peace in which we came be reflected in the lives of all mankind." The astronauts splashed down on December 19, 1972. Pundits suggested that Apollo was just a precursor to the establishment of a lunar base and a human colony on the moon, but that never happened. Kennedy's dream was realized, but many others' were shattered. The moon was abandoned. The future was cancelled.

Top: Astronaut Eugene A. Cernan, Apollo 17 mission commander, taking a spin in the Lunar Roving Vehicle, known affectionately as the moon buggy, at the Taurus-Littrow landing site. The photograph was taken by geologist–astronaut Harrison H. Schmitt, Lunar Module pilot.

Left: Detail of one of a series of powerful images of an abandoned rocket facility at White Sands, New Mexico, USA, 1980, captured by Magnum photographer René Burri.

Right: Verner Panton, Bar, Spiegel Publishing House, Hamburg, Germany, 1969.

02 "A question of living tomorrow"

With hindsight the lasting impact of space travel on our domestic environment might easily be reduced to Velcro fasteners and Teflon non-stick pans. However, for a brief period at the height of the race to the moon there were genuine signs that life on earth would never be the same again.

Events in outer space triggered a craze on the ground for all things futuristic. Designers from different disciplines began creating ultra-modern furniture, clothes and even houses for the space-age consumer. This period witnessed the evolution of a space-inspired "look", which mirrored the styling of metallic satellites, the orbiting patterns of spacecraft and the distinctive shape of astronauts' helmets. Technological innovation also brought a sense of rediscovery in the most everyday activities. It was as if we all had another chance at childhood, an opportunity to start over using a new set of rules, and remake the future.

The years following World War II saw the rapid development of industrially manufactured furniture. Designers including Charles Eames, Eero Saarinen, and Jean Prouvé applied industrial methods and materials to domestic products and architecture. Saarinen's *Tulip* chair (1956) and TWA Terminal (1956–62) at John F. Kennedy airport, New York, saw the marrying of organic forms with industrial production, as did the Theme Building (1962) at Los Angeles International Airport. This trend was adopted by a new generation of designers who revolutionized the domestic landscape in the new era of space travel.

Science proved to be a major influence on domestic design in the 1950s, the era associated with the atomic bomb. Motifs taken from atomic physics decorated everything from tableware to cocktail accessories. The amorphous blobs, seen everywhere from fabric patterns to coffee tables, were inspired by images of tiny living cells as seen through a microscope. Aerodynamic fins appeared on cars and kitchen appliances in a celebration of jet-powered air travel. 1950s design reflected the technological achievements of the time and embodied an optimistic attitude to the future, a spirit that would be developed in many different ways.

Left: Aerodynamic fins, inspired by the advent of jet-powered air travel, appeared on products as diverse as automobiles and kitchen appliances in the 1950s. Design in the post-war era was inspired by new technology and this set the precedent for what was to come in the space age.

The reorganization of wartime munitions and aircraft factories had led to an abundance of aluminum products appearing on the market in the 1940s and 1950s. Aluminum also became the material of choice for some of the earliest product designs to be inspired by the conquest of space. The *Arco* lamp (1962) designed by Achille and Giacomo Castiglioni, resembles the shiny, spherical form of the very first Sputnik. The lamp hangs from a slender metallic arm, which arcs from a base on the floor as if thrusting into orbit. *Arco* appears to defy gravity, hovering in space. It is one of many lamps that appeared in the early years of the space age and heralds the introduction of the space-age style into domestic design. Similar models include the *Topan* (1959) pendant lamp designed by Verner Panton and manufactured by Louis Poulsen.

Aluminum may have been used for the first satellites, but it was plastic that brought a whole new dimension to modern living. Plastic, in all its various guises, defined the style of the space age. New methods of molding and joining plastics arrived at just the right time for designers hoping to celebrate the new possibilities of the space age. Paco Rabanne was one such designer. He entered the Parisian fashion scene in the mid-1960s after initial training as an architect. In his earliest collections he ditched the use of needle and thread to experiment instead with different methods of constructing garments. This involved taking small squares of aluminum and a plastic known as Rhodoid, and linking them together with metal rings to create futuristic clothes that barely covered the body. The use of white Rhodoid and reflective aluminum, the colors most associated with the space age, added to his outfits' futuristic appearance.

Paco Rabanne loved plastic: here was a cheap, colorful and lightweight material that was free of any association with the fashions of the past. His first experiments with Rhodoid resulted in oversized, Op-Art-style earrings, which were a big hit on their release in 1965. A short time later, Paco Rabanne applied the plastic used in these accessories to the creation of whole outfits. He rejected the soft, luxurious fabrics of high fashion and chose instead to "build" outfits from hard materials that had more in common with engineering construction than couture.

He described his first manifesto collection as "unwearable dresses in contemporary materials." When it was presented at the Georges V Hotel in Paris, February, 1966, the show was greeted with the mixed reactions of outrage and applause that became synonymous with his subsequent creations. His next outing was particularly riotous. The show was staged at the Crazy Horse Saloon, a racy Parisian theater, where the designer employed the resident strippers to present his "unwearable"

Right: Eero Saarinen, *Tulip* chair, 1956. Saarinen's marrying of organic shapes with industrial materials had a great influential on a new generation of furniture designers.

clothes. The troupe performed a classic striptease routine while wearing Paco Rabanne's futuristic fashions. It was an appropriate way for Paco Rabanne to present his outfits since the chain-linked squares of Rhodoid and aluminum barely covered the model's bodies at all. With this collection he challenged the notion that clothes should hide the body and his choice of venue foreshadowed the increasingly overt use of sex in fashion and advertising.

"My clothes are weapons," remarked Paco Rabanne in a 1967 issue of *Marie Claire* magazine. With his arsenal of ultra-cool apparel, Rabanne launched an attack against the use of delicate materials in high fashion and blazed a trail towards alternative methods of production. A prime example of this is his Paper Dresses collection of 1967. Paper was already being championed as a revolutionary clothing material, particularly in the USA where it was applied to functional work wear. Paco Rabanne chose not to treat paper as merely a cheap alternative to textiles. He regarded it as a material in its own right and formulated various means of joining different panels of Nylon-reinforced paper together. Again he shunned stitching, preferring instead to use colored adhesive tape which became a prominent element in the garment's design.

In the years before environmental awareness, it was suggested that disposable paper clothes might evolve into a fashion staple of the future. Since World War II, such single-use commodities were considered to be the way forward. NASA's Saturn V was the ultimate symbol of the throwaway society—in both size and expense. Millions of dollars were invested in this gargantuan rocket, but like a paper napkin, it could only be used once. Writing at the time, Alvin Toffler, a prominent social theorist, regarded paper clothing as a logical progression in the trend for disposable goods. In his 1970 book *Future Shock* he writes: "Products created for short-term or one-time use are becoming more numerous and crucial to our

Top: Charles Luckman, William Pereira, Welton Becket, and Paul R. Williams, Theme Building, Los Angeles International Airport, Los Angeles, USA, 1962.

way of life. The recent introduction of paper and quasi-paper clothing carried the trend towards disposability a step further. Fashionable boutiques and working-class clothing stores have sprouted whole departments devoted to gaily colored and imaginatively designed paper apparel." Fashion items, by their very nature, have a short-term existence and paper clothing, such as that designed by Paco Rabanne, sought to cut this life-span even further. Being practical and inexpensive are not always top priorities in the fashion business and the trend never really caught on, but, Paco Rabanne's Paper Dresses nevertheless enjoyed considerable success.

An equally radical yet less successful venture for Paco Rabanne was the *Giffo* raincoat (design 1965, prototype 1968). With *Giffo*, Paco Rabanne again tried to make fashion more accessible by speeding up the production process and reducing costs. *Giffo* was unusual in that it was a garment created from a single piece of material with no stitching or join of any kind. To make the coat, liquid plastic was sprayed into a specially shaped mold, allowed to set for a few seconds, then it was removed and ready to wear. Despite substantial investment, the manufacturing process that created *Giffo* was a commercial failure and the design never made it past the prototype phase.

Paco Rabanne, like other designers of that era, found great motivation in making quality design—once the sole preserve of the wealthy—available to the mass market. Synthetic materials such as plastic and foam aided this process. The desire to manufacture products in a single operation—thus reducing the cost of production—became an obsession for several forward-thinking designers. Verner Panton, for example, spent years perfecting his *Panton* chair (design 1958–67, production 1967) before it was unveiled as the first chair to be molded from a single piece of plastic. The *Panton* chair, with its sleek lines and dynamic form, is a monument to new technology and its unique shape is derived directly from the industrial process used in its manufacture. The chair is at once confident, sexy, seductive, and even though it is completely synthetic, the *Panton* chair feels natural and ergonomically shaped. This marrying of smooth, organic form with an industrial manufacturing process is typical of space-age design. Machine-made furniture could remain true to its materials and production without looking hard and unnatural.

A further example of this approach is evident in the work of Finnish designer Eero Aarnio. His *Ball* chair (design 1963) is a spherical seating unit fashioned out of fiberglass. The shape of the chair and the material used had not before been witnessed in the furniture industry. The *Bubble* chair (1968) is of a similar shape but made from transparent acrylic and hangs from the ceiling. Both chairs appear to float in

Left: Paco Rabanne, (clockwise from top left) Aluminum mini-dress, 1967–68; *Giffo* raincoat, design 1965, prototype 1968; Paper dress, 1967.

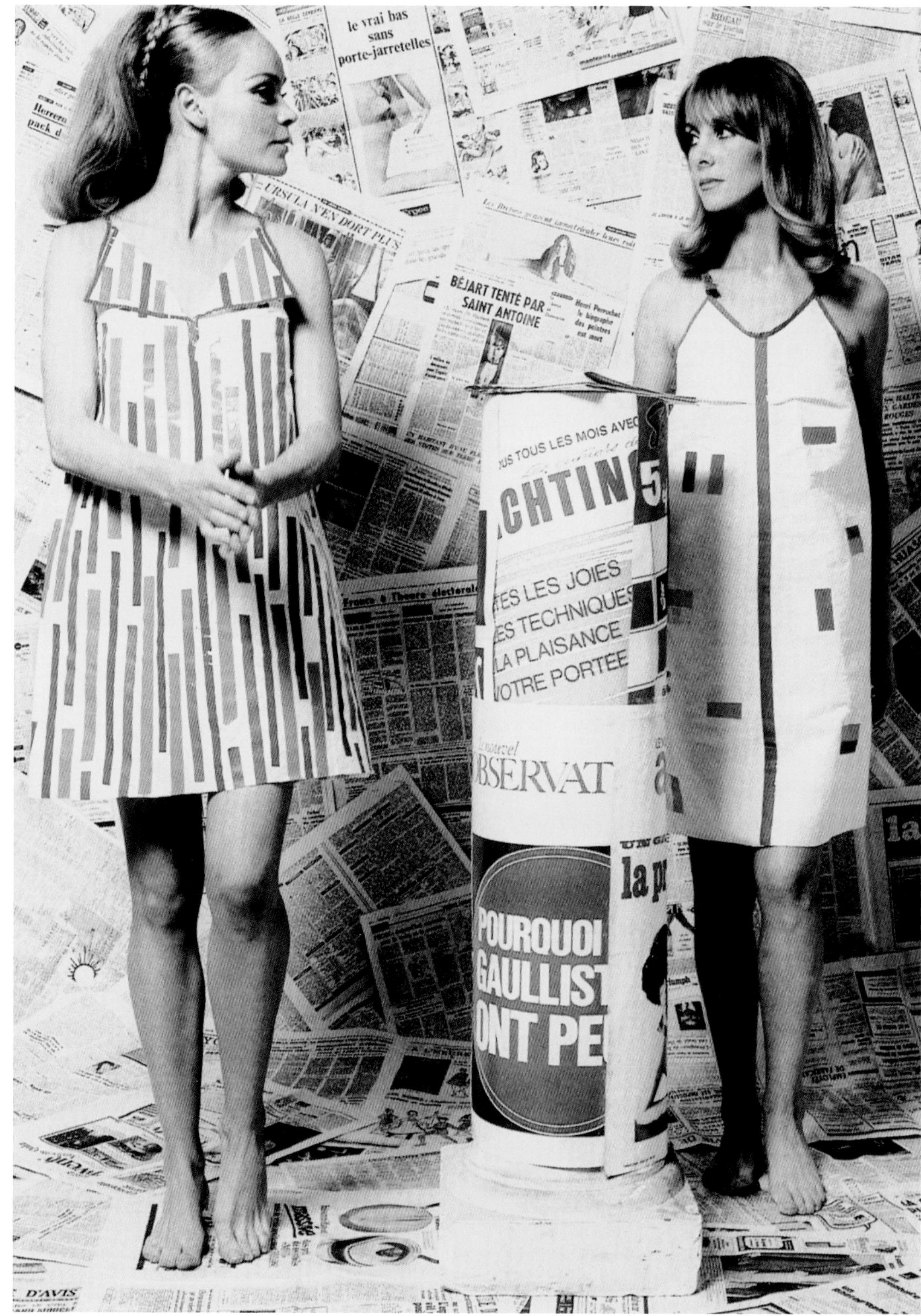

Right: Paco Rabanne, Paper dresses, 1967.

Opposite, top to bottom: Eero Aarnio, *Bubble* chair, 1968; *Pastil* chair, 1967; and *Tomato* chair, 1971.

mid-air and embody the space-age phenomenon of zero gravity. Their clean, spherical form resembles an astronaut's helmet and marks a departure from the sharp, rigid shapes of the past. Aarnio's *Pastil* chair (1967) and *Tomato* chair (1971) continue this radical approach and can be used both inside and outdoors. Aarnio's chairs ultimately invite leisurely relaxation; they are designed for lounging. None of these chairs look man-made, or the product of traditional manufacture. Their smooth, globular forms appear to have landed from outer space.

The *Panton*, *Bubble*, *Tomato*, and *Pastil* chairs are a radical break with history. They clash with the rectangular shapes of the typical home and stand out as novelty objects. These plastic chairs needed an environment to match their space-age form, a home where they could sit in harmony with their surroundings. They did not have to wait long for its arrival. The conquest of space and talk of establishing a colony on the moon triggered much debate about the home of the future. The discovery of a new world—the moon—brought with it the opportunity to start afresh. The question of tomorrow's home took on greater significance and became the subject of increasing curiosity. An early space-age residence was John Lautner's Chemosphere (1960). Shaped like a flying saucer it seemed to hover among the Los Angeles hills, but it was built with traditional materials and was obviously of this earth. Nevertheless, with its futuristic styling and unusual shape, Chemosphere was still a daring departure from the traditional home. The typical house was a rectangular box sitting on the floor, but Chemosphere dispenses with that notion and opens up a living space while also suspending it some way above the ground.

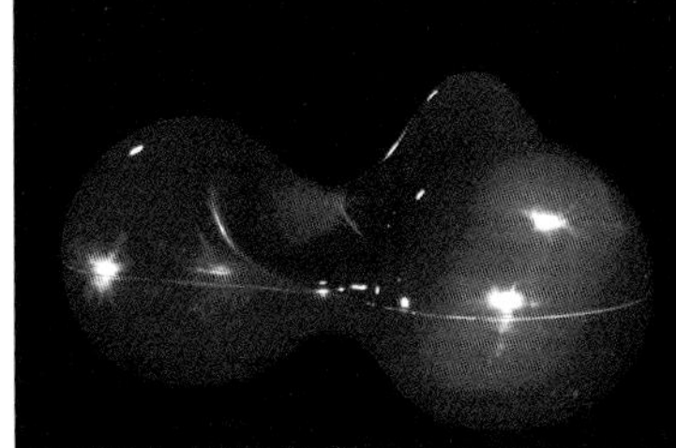

In 1968, the home of tomorrow arrived. Finnish architect Matti Suuronen first designed Futuro, a flying-saucer-shaped residence, as a transportable ski cabin. The ellipsoid shell was made up of sixteen plastic panels and rested on a framework of spindly legs. The exterior and interior skins were manufactured from glass-reinforced polyester (GRP) with an insulating layer of polyurethane. All interior elements, including the kitchen and furniture, were also made with GRP, while the windows were perspex. Futuro was yet another example of space-age design's obsession with creating bulky forms with relatively little weight.

Had Futuro remained a chic ski cabin or fashionable hideaway, it might have proved successful. However, the marketing team behind it had much bigger ideas. The futuristic house was hyped as the dawn of a whole new way of living. Promotional material pictured whole apartment blocks and stacking hotels that used Futuro as an accommodation module. A huge publicity campaign saw Futuro tour the world and production licences were sold in twenty-four different countries.

The house sailed into London on board a ship promoting Finnish exports, but, in the USA, it was to receive an even grander premiere. A ready-made Futuro was to be flown into Washington D.C. hanging beneath a helicopter. The stunt emphasized the Futuro's similarities to a spacecraft, but it also had a practical purpose. The house was designed to be moved easily from place to place. Its primary function as a ski cabin meant that it would be located in mountain ranges with little or no access, and this was always a prominent factor in its design. Futuro responded to the needs of an increasingly mobile society because it could be assembled away from its specified site and delivered to it later. Unfortunately, on the day of Futuro's American launch, there were no helicopters available that were powerful enough to fly the house over the city and into the press arena. Most were fighting the war in Vietnam and the one that was to be used had suffered a malfunction. Such obstacles seemed to dog Futuro wherever it went and the house failed to live up to its promises.

As if to confirm the notion that plastic homes were the way of the future, a number of houses similar to Futuro appeared around the same time. The pod-like Futurotel (1966), a two-story accommodation space, was designed in the Netherlands for the Krasnapolsky Hotel, Amsterdam. Its most prominent feature was a large window that looked like the eye of a huge bug. The Spharoid (1967), designed by Guy de Moreau, appeared in Belgium and in Switzerland, architects Casoni & Casoni created the spherical holiday house, Rondo (1969). Additionally, in France, there were the Egg Houses (1965) designed by Hausermann, Camoletti & Hoechel for Vinner & Co., Paris, and Jean Maneval's Six Shell Bubble House (1968). This holiday house, also made from GRP, was formed by joining together six separate, self-supporting units, which could be transported on the back of a truck. It

was originally designed as accommodation for an experimental resort in the Pyrenean mountains. Six Shell Bubble House went into commercial production in 1968, but ended only two years later and only about thirty homes were ever made.

There were plenty of opportunities to buy into the space-age lifestyle for those whose budgets could not stretch to a plastic house. Vico Magistretti's *Eclisse* lamp (1965) enabled space-age consumers to create their own bedside lunar eclipse. The simple yet refined shape consisted of three half spheres—one for the base, the second to shield the bulb, and a third to adjust the flow of light. The lamp works like a solar eclipse. The adjustable half-sphere rotates to block the flow of light like the moon blocking the light from the sun.

Computers—once huge, room-filling machines—shrunk in size and crossed into the realm of entertainment with one of the first video arcade games, *Computer Space*. (1971) Its unique plastic

Left: John Lautner, Chemosphere, Los Angeles, USA, 1960.

Right: Matti Suuronen, Futuro house, Finland, 1968.

1234567890

casing is completely different from any of the crate-like video game machines that followed it. The shape of the *Computer Space* console resembles a simplified figure holding out the game's control panel, as if to say "play me." The actual game demonstrates the ability of electronic media to engage people and provide a unique experience. *Computer Space*, no matter how basic it looks today, was the origin of the video-game phenomenon, which has grown to be one of the biggest enterprises in the world. Computers also spawned an assortment of ultra-modern typefaces such as *OCR-A* (1966) and *OCR-B* (1968) developed by the European Computer Manufacturers Association and Adrian Frutiger, Wim Crouwel's *New Alphabet* (1967), and *E13B* developed by the American Bankers Association (mid-1960s). Although these typefaces were largely developed to be read by electronic devices in banks and other institutions, their futuristic style soon caught on. Letraset released Colin Brignall's *Countdown*, which resembled the new computer-readable type. Graphic designers used the new typefaces on record sleeves, magazines, and anywhere else that called for a futuristic aesthetic.

Plastic casings for television sets were shaped to imitate an astronaut's headgear, as demonstrated by JVC's *Videosphere* (1970) and Panasonic's *Model TR-05* (1972). The *Videocapsule* (1972), also by JVC, resembled a lunar rover and had a flip-top screen. This was a far cry from the days when television was first introduced to the home and the casings were made to look like antique wooden cabinets. Record players, too, such as the *22 GF 303/03L* (1970) manufactured by Philips, and

COUNTDOWN

1234567890

Top: *CMC7*, early 1960s; Wim Crouwel, *New Alphabet*, 1967.

Center: Colin Brignall, *Countdown*, for Letraset, mid–1960s. Letraset's instant dry transfer lettering added to the trend for experimentation and informality in design.

Bottom: American Bankers' Association, *E13B*, mid–1960s. A computer-readable typeface developed for use in the financial sector, which can still be seen on many checkbooks.

Right: Jean Maneval, La Bulle Six Coques (Six Shell Bubble House), 1968.

CONFIDENTIEL par Jacques Chancel

VOUS AUREZ BIENTOT VOTRE SOUCOUPE VOLANTE

Une soucoupe qui est... une maison. Avec petit escalier extérieur et tout et tout.

LES Pyrénées n'en avaient jamais tant vu... A Gripp la Mongie, les skieurs du col du Tourmalet ont découvert, hier, un monde inconnu. Près du torrent, des soucoupes volantes d'un style tout à fait nouveau paradaient en bon ordre derrière les sapinettes. Etrange non ?

Regardez notre photo ci-dessus et vous comprendrez aisément qu'il y avait de quoi s'étonner. Il est des rencontres qui provoquent un choc. La surprise, toutefois, n'a pas fait long feu. Quelques

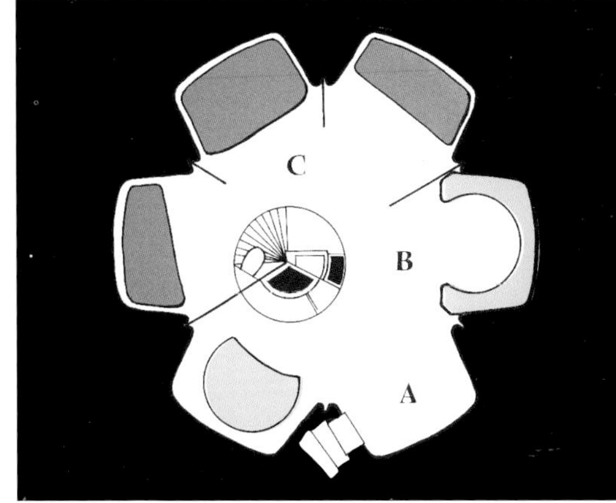

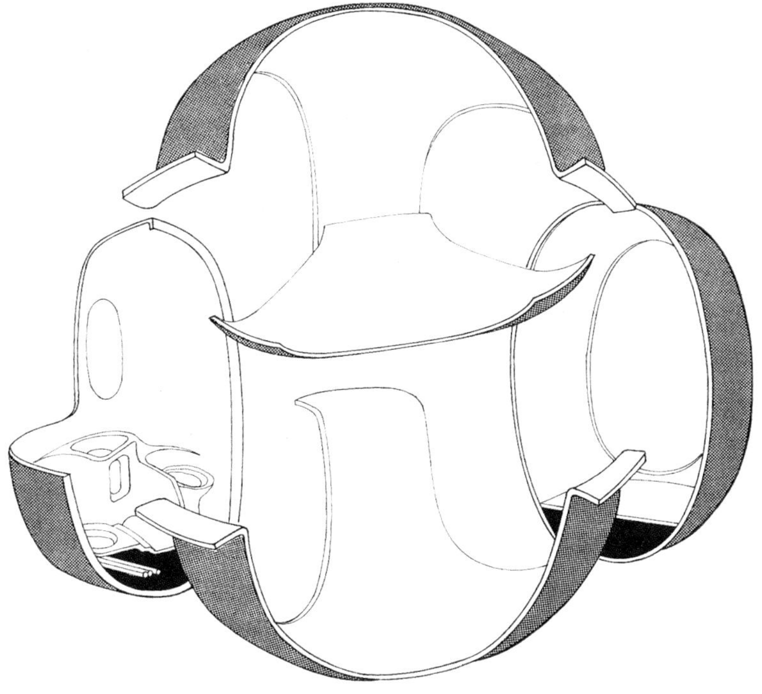

The French architect and urbanist Jean Maneval (1923–86) was the first to create a living unit entirely of man-made materials and mass-produced for the commercial market. Designed in 1964 and produced from 1968 by Batiplastique, Maneval's Six Shell Bubble provided the housing for an experimental holiday village nestling in the Pyrenees. This settlement comprised 20 identical bubble houses which were factory-made and required the minimum of on-site installation work. Their forms and colors (white, green, chestnut brown) were designed to blend perfectly into the landscape. Each unit is made of 6 shells connected by waterproof, flexible joints. These are suspended from a metal frame which rests on a concrete base supporting the floor. A hemispherical cap tops the whole thing off. The shells are made from polyester reinforced with methacrylate. The living area comprises around 32 m^2, and the weight of each unit is 200 kg. Each bubble has its own integral furniture designed in wood and metal by Maneval and adapted to the curved forms of the shells. Production of the bubble houses stopped in 1970 and in total only around 30 were made. Nevertheless press coverage of the time heralded their arrival in the sleepy village of Gripp as the opportunity to "have your own flying saucer."

Right: Nolan Bushnell for Nutting and Associates, *Computer Space*, 1971. This was the first stand-alone computer console with the single purpose of game playing. The game takes place in outer space, where the player has to battle in a rocket ship against two flying saucers. Few knew what to make of the machine on its release in 1971, but Bushnell, the game's originator, later went on to enormous success as the founder of gaming giant, Atari.

Weltron's *Model 2001* (1970), adopted space-age styling, but, more importantly, they became ever more portable and provided music on the go in an era of increased mobility.

Even personal hygiene was given the futuristic treatment with the unveiling in 1970 of Sanyo Electric Corporation's *Ultrasonic Bath*. This "human washing machine" was described in the firm's accompanying literature as "truly the fully automatic bath of the future." To operate it, all one had to do was "select the desired water temperature and push a button." The machine then "soaks, washes, and rinses the human body in an abundance of lather produced by ultrasonic waves", and finally, "dries and massages the body."

Plastic had certainly made an impact in the age of space travel. It was a boom time for the industry and NASA set the standard when it came to investing in research and development. Lighter, tougher, and safer synthetic materials were required all the time in the mission to reach the moon. The human race had defied the laws of

Left: Vico Magistretti, *Eclisse* lamp, 1965.

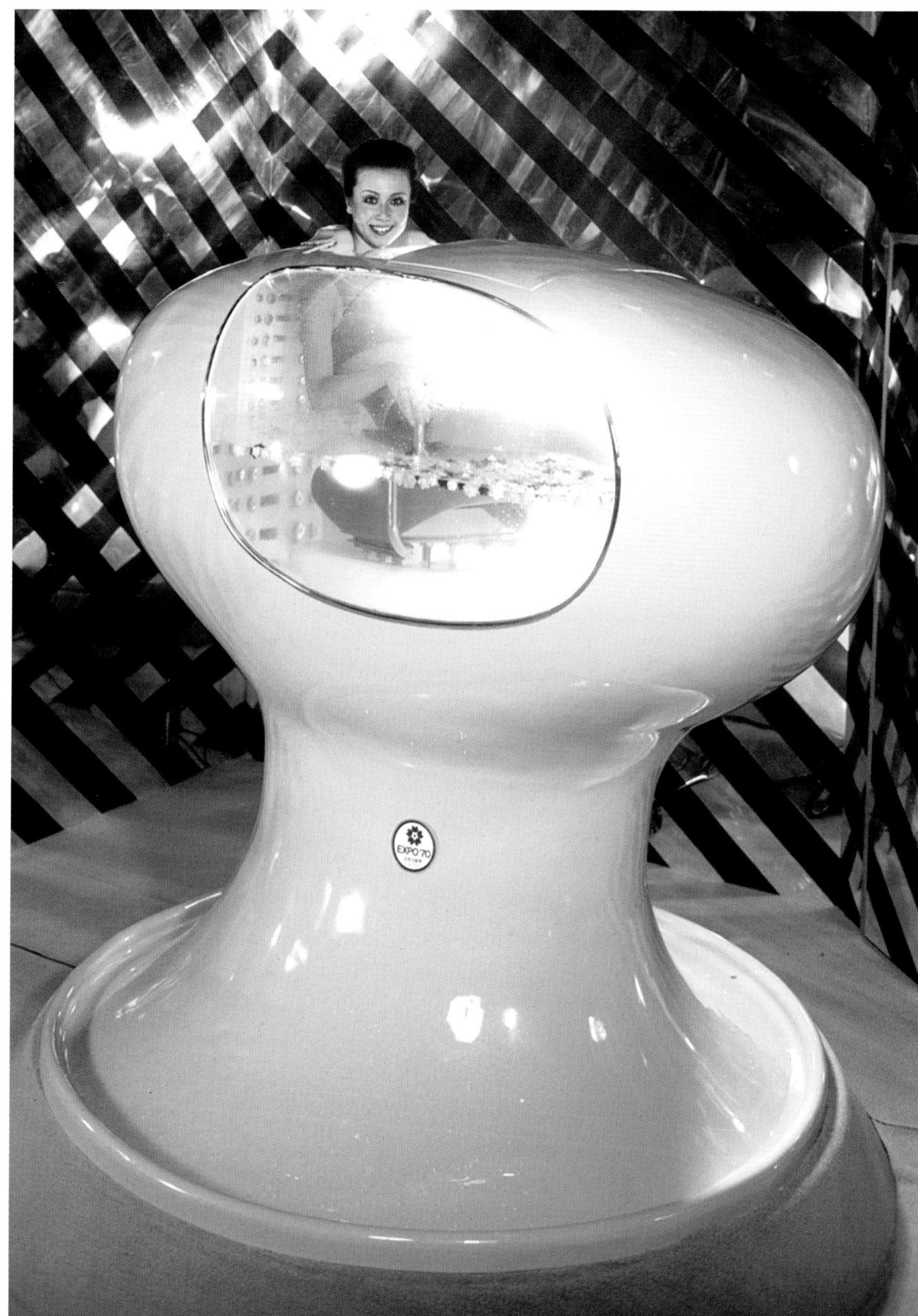

Right: Sanyo Electric Corporation, *Ultrasonic Bath*, 1970. Often referred to as the "human washing machine" this contraption was described in its promotional literature as "truly the fully automatic bath of the future."

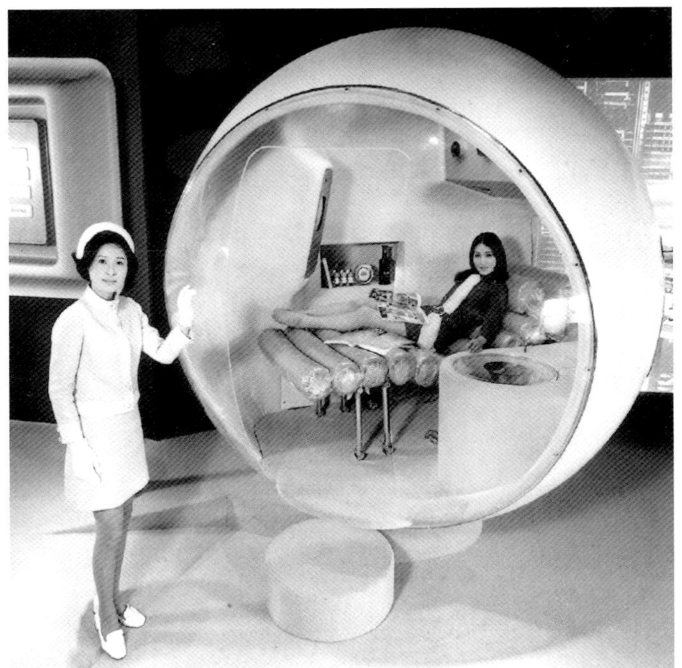

gravity by sending satellites and people into space. When Gagarin became the first person in space, the Supreme Soviet declared it as "an unparalleled victory of man over the forces of nature." Now, with the development of synthetic plastics, man scored another victory over nature and was free to shape his own environment without the use of natural materials such as wood, leather, and stone.

Household objects gradually became less precious and our relationships to them less formal. For perhaps the first time in history it became cheaper to replace furniture and fittings than it did to repair them. Indeed, the complex processes used in the manufacture of plastic products did not lend themselves to home maintenance in the same way wood does. This notion of replacing products rather than repairing them was a further indicator of the move toward a throwaway society and encouraged yet more consumer spending—and even more waste.

However, one of the biggest problems with the new throwaway plastic products was that they were actually very difficult to dispose of. Plastic did not decompose and could not be incinerated because of the noxious gases it discharged. Concern for the environment grew in the early 1970s and the perils of plastic became increasingly clear. The overconsumption of the 1960s was questioned, and then the oil crisis of 1973 put an end to any notions of a plastic future. The price of crude oil quadrupled after the Organisation of Petroleum Exporting Countries (OPEC) reduced its supply, and the cost of plastic rocketed as a result. It was followed by a severe international recession, which made the throwaway attitude of the 1960s seem irresponsible.

Production of the *Panton* chair—the very pinnacle of plastic design—was halted in the USA in 1975 after complaints that the plastic used to make it was not as durable as was first thought. Natural materials became popular once more and plastic was deemed cheap and ecologically unsound. Worries about the environment escalated as the oil crisis deepened and made people aware of how vulnerable the world was in its reliance on technologies fuelled by a limited resource. The plastic bubble had burst.

Top: Sanyo Electric Corporation, *Living Capsule*, 1970. The concept of capsule living was a favorite of the space age. This insulated, spherical room came with its own anatomically constructed bed, color TV, video-telephone, stereo, and bar.

Right: Verner Panton, *Panton* chair, design 1958–67, production 1968. It was the first chair to be molded from a single piece of plastic.

Space exploration ushered in an era of transformations and this is expressed in the fashions of the day. The fashionable female silhouette evolved from the curvaceous, flowing, mature figure that was typical of the 1950s, to a skinny, angular, androgynous look with an emphasis on youth. The traditional conventions of dress were overturned by a new and practical style well suited to the needs of modern living. The very first spacewalk by cosmonaut Alexei Leonov and the subsequent excursion by Edward White are ultimate examples of the human race entering an age of previously unimaginable mobility. Such activity called for a completely new wardrobe for use in outer space. The EVA outfit worn by Leonov on his spacewalk had to protect him from the harshest environment a human being had ever encountered as well as possess enough flexibility to permit him to maneuver safely in space.

The primary need for freedom of movement in the wardrobe for outer space was also expressed in the futuristic outfits by fashion designers André Courrèges and Pierre Cardin. Their collections from the mid-1960s to the early 1970s provided space-age consumers with a style and spirit appropriate to their time. Arguably André Courrèges was the inventor of the miniskirt. This once outrageous garment not only uncovered the female figure, but also liberated it for greater movement. A headline in a March 1965 issue of *Colour* magazine, a supplement to the *Observer* newspaper, announced Courrèges's dynamic styling of miniskirts, trapeze dresses, catsuits, and tunics as the "clothes of the future." Joy Tagney, the author of the piece, described how Courrèges's garments were often referred to as "space-age" clothes, but, as she points out, "this doesn't mean bizarre pressure suits and odd helmets, it means clothes for the space

Above: Livio Castiglioni and Gianfranco Frattini, *Boalum* lamp, Artemide, Italy, 1970. Made with flexible, translucent plastic tubing, the *Boalum* lamp could be twisted into all kinds of different shapes, which allowed its user to define its final design.

age: the age of action, freedom, and participation." Courrèges's clothes are cut for movement. In the Joy Tagney interview Courrèges states: "I don't make clothes for women who lead an unreal, pampered life, but for girls who go shopping, run for buses." His comment expresses a desire to cater for casual everyday wear rather than opulent formal attire, a shift that echoes the move in domestic environments toward a more relaxed style of living. The precise styling of his clothes also adheres to properties of new synthetic fabrics and the advanced technology employed in their manufacture.

The Courrèges look is svelte and sparse, but also youthful and optimistic. Silver (representing for Courrèges the moon), white (light), and azure blue (the cosmos) make regular appearances in the Courrèges palette. The cosmonaut-style collections of the mid-1960s were always topped with a hat to balance the proportions of his designs. On occasion the hat would reach down over the face and act as a visor across the eyes, leaving only a narrow strip to see through. This slit motif also occurs in an example of Courrèges's futuristic eyewear from a collection of spring/summer 1965. Here it provides a slender peep-hole through a pair of otherwise solid, white plastic goggles.

The noisy catwalk shows where André Courrèges unveiled his sharply tailored outfits were frenetic ordeals that complemented the dynamic nature of his clothes. "His shows are startling experiences" recounts Joy Tagney. She later describes how the models, "march on and off like robots, giving themselves just enough time to display the clothes with quick, jerky movements." Like the Italian Futurists and the Russian Constructivists of the early 20th century, Courrèges was progressive in his outlook and advocated the use of high technology to create a style that is truly representative of its era.

In the 1960s, Pierre Cardin was also heavily influenced by the arrival of space travel. He once stated that his greatest achievement was to have worn and walked in the same spacesuit that Neil Armstrong wore on the moon. Cardin's Cosmos range, released in 1966, employed a basic unisex design, which could be adapted to accommodate every member of the family. Again, like the outfits by Courrèges, the Cosmos range was practical and allied to mobility. The basic ensemble consisted of a pinafore or short tunic worn over a tight-fitting sweater. The male variation was completed by trousers and a peaked cap, whereas the female version incorporated tights and was topped by a domed, felt hat or hood. The Cosmos range was not as stark as the collection presented by Courrèges and included novel details such as epaulets, which gave it the quasi-military look of a space cadet's uniform.

Elle magazine proclaimed Cardin's next collection, Cosmocorps, the essential look for 1967. As with his

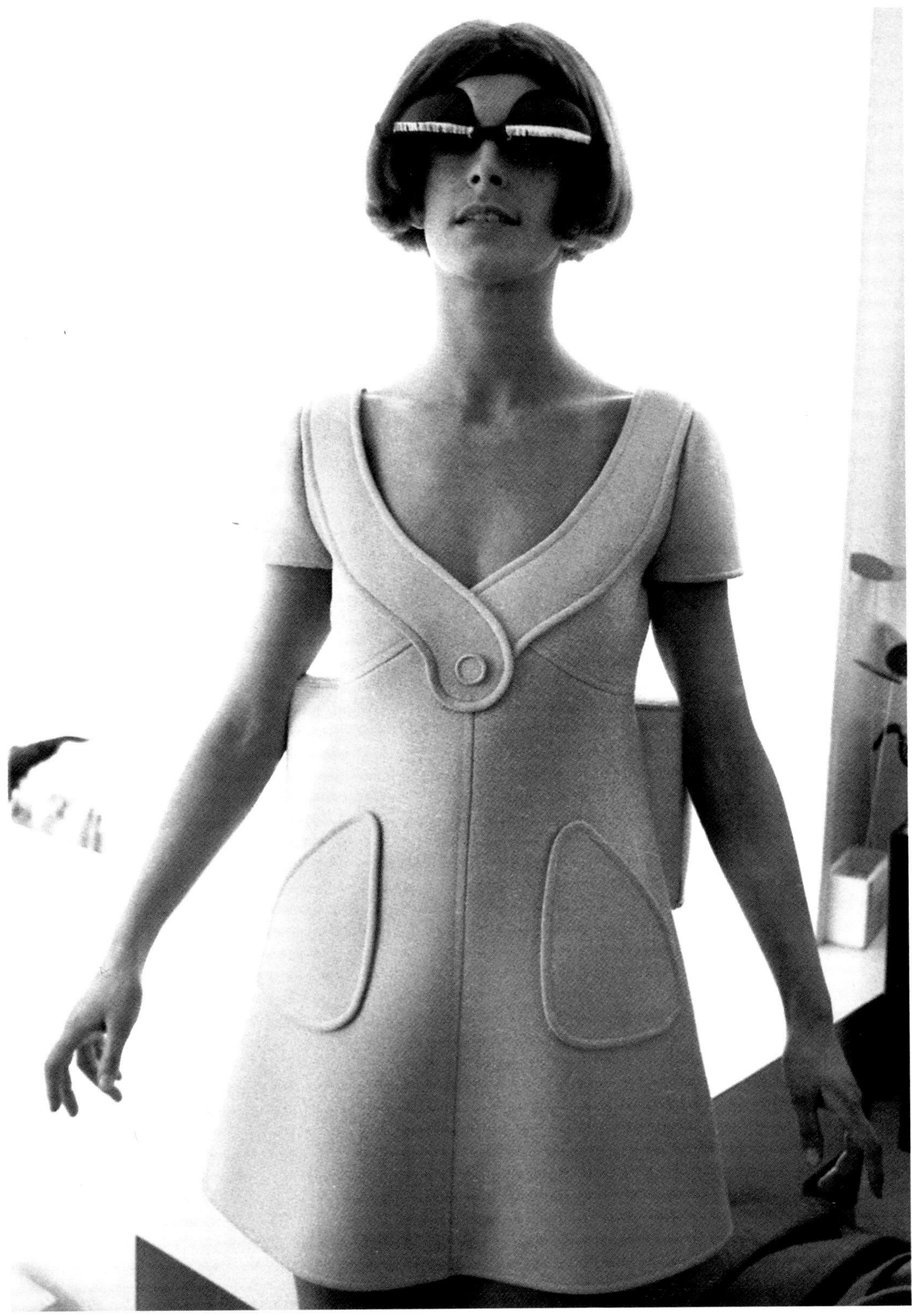

Left: Courrèges, spring/summer collection, 1965.

Top: Pierre Cardin, *Cosmocorps*, 1967.

previous collection, Cardin made this range adaptable so it could be transformed from casual day wear to smart evening attire. This collection, like the first, was also brightly colored and heavily decorated, most obviously with the PC monogram emblazoned across the chest. The total effect, despite being comfortable and practical, proved too outlandish for the mass market. However, simplified replicas of the collection soon appeared on the streets in fashionable shopping districts across Europe and the USA.

Pierre Cardin embraced the future and celebrated the arrival of the space age. At the time, he said of his work: "The clothes that I prefer are those I invent for a life that doesn't exist yet—the world of tomorrow." He applied his space-age styling to spectacular eyewear as well as other accessories and even to whole interiors, as seen in his theater, Espace Pierre Cardin (1970), and Antti Lovag's Palais Bulle [Bubble Palace] which Cardin bought in the 1980s.

In the past, style had been dictated by the wealthy, but now it was responding to the needs of the young, mass market. Pierre Cardin, André Courrèges, and Paco Rabanne all acknowledged a shift in the priorities of the fashion business. They also helped redefine the female silhouette from the feminine and curvaceous shape made popular in the 1950s, to the skinny, boyish figure that has come to be associated with the fashion models of the 1960s. In his own way, each designer contributed to the overthrow of conventional practices in the fashion industry. In many respects, the successes in space made it acceptable to challenge traditional methods and beliefs. It was new technology that first put a cosmonaut into orbit and it was a similar convention-defying attitude that landed an astronaut on the moon. Space travel, with its spectacular successes arising from new and untried means, legitimized and even encouraged experimentation in other areas of life and creativity.

Italian designer Cesare "Joe" Colombo injected that same spirit of experimentation into the home. The philosophy behind most of his work emphasized progress and change. His designs are not especially futuristic in style, but the attitude they

promote is wholly in tune with the youthfulness of the space age. This hugely influential figure enjoyed a short yet prolific period as a designer after embarking initially on a career as a painter and sculptor. His father manufactured electrical equipment and when he fell ill in 1958, Joe Colombo and his brother, Gianni, took charge of the family business. It was in his father's factory that Colombo began experimenting with the latest plastics and production processes that came to have such an influence on his work as a designer. In 1962, he established a studio in Milan and set to the task of revolutionizing the modern home.

Colombo spoke of the enormous possibilities presented by developments in communication technologies and suggested that, in the near future, people might live, work, and study at home. For these people he created a new type of habitat consisting of "spaces that can be transformed, spaces conducive to meditation and experi-mentation, to intimacy and to interpersonal exchanges." Colombo's commitment to a fluid and dynamic lifestyle stretched from whole habitation capsules down to compact storage systems and individual chairs. The *Tube* chair (1969), manufactured by Flexform, comprises of four upholstered cylinders of varying diameter, which can be hooked together to form a seating unit. The chair was sold in a drawstring bag with the four cylinders slotted neatly inside each other to minimize storage space. Space-saving devices were a passion of Colombo's and he was meticulous in searching out new ways of reducing an object's storage requirements. The philosophy behind *Tube* chair was applied to a series of interior environments where multi-function units and foldaway furniture made the most of a limited amount of space.

The *Roto-Living-Unit* (1969) and *Cabriolet-Bed* (1969) were invented as tools for the new lifestyle of the space age. The unusual design of the *Cabriolet-Bed* responded to the need for privacy in an open-plan apartment. A retractable canopy could be lowered down over the large bed to create an intimate space secluded from the rest of the dwelling. A more luxurious manifestation of Colombo's ideas for capsule living was exhibited

Top: Pierre Cardin, *Cosmocorps*, 1967.

Right and **opposite:** Antti Lovag, Palais Bulle [Bubble Palace], 1975, bought in 1989 by Pierre Cardin.

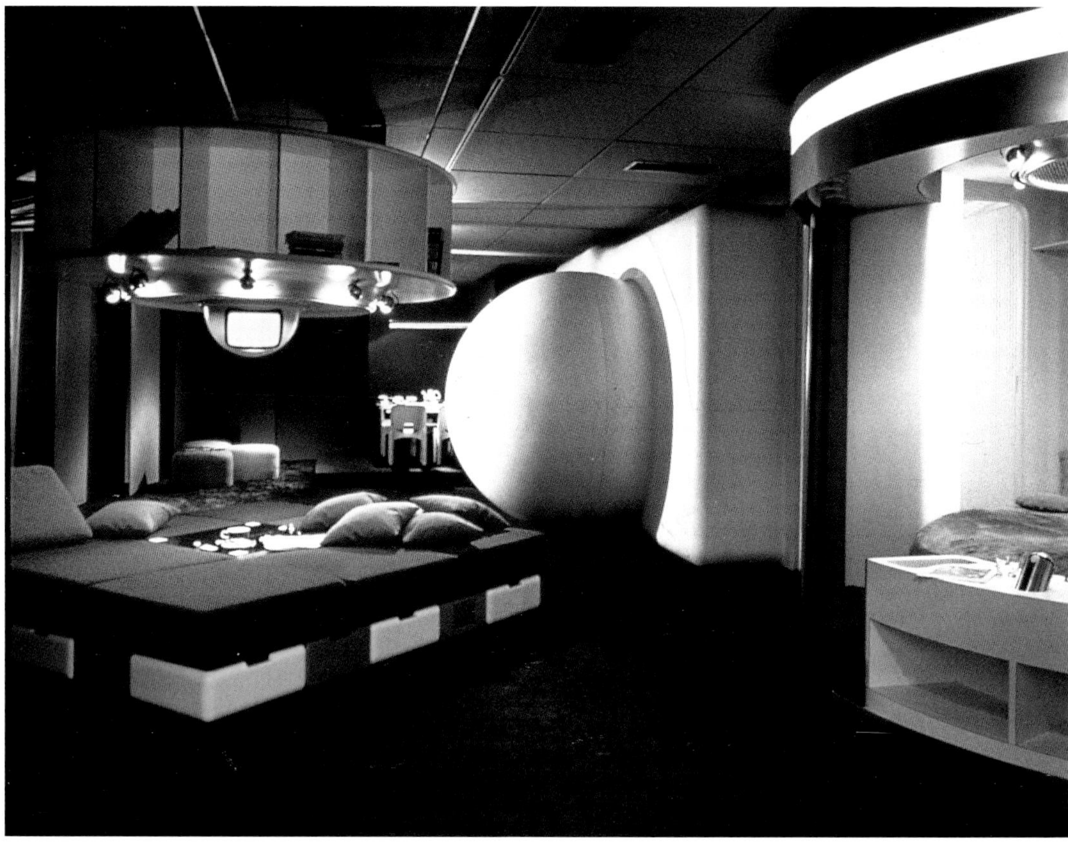

Top: Joe Colombo, *Habitation Capsule*, exhibited at Visiona 1, Cologne Furniture Fair, 1969.

under the banner of Visiona 1, at the Cologne Furniture Fair of 1969. In this prototype dwelling, known as the *Habitation Capsule* (1969), Colombo employed a whole range of new synthetic materials to create a fluid space fitted with all the facilities of a modern home. *Habitation Capsule* looked just as futuristic as the ideas it embodied. The inviting bed was particularly prominent and sat below a circular shelving unit complete with a spherical TV set, which echoed the globular form of the central living cell.

Colombo's various inventions for capsule living transformed the home into an interior not unlike the cabin of a sea-faring yacht. The yachtsman is constantly tending to the needs of his craft and transforms its state in response to the conditions and environment it encounters. Anyone using one of Colombo's adaptable units would act in a similar manner and constantly modify his environment depending on the activity he wished to undertake. This was quite a departure from the usual approach to interiors in the West, and had more in common with the flexibility of the traditional Japanese home.

Total Furnishing Unit (1971), one of Colombo's last works, was commissioned by the Museum of Modern Art in New York for its 1972 retrospective of Italian design, *Italy: The New Domestic Landscape*. The museum invited a selection of well-known Italian designers to explore the changing domestic landscape and translate their ideas into physical designs. One of the chief concerns behind the design of *Total Furnishing Unit* was to create a dwelling that was better suited to the ever-changing needs of the consumer of the future, a new type of interior that would make optimum use of their time and space. Colombo sought to achieve this through four different "furnishing units," which made up the kitchen,

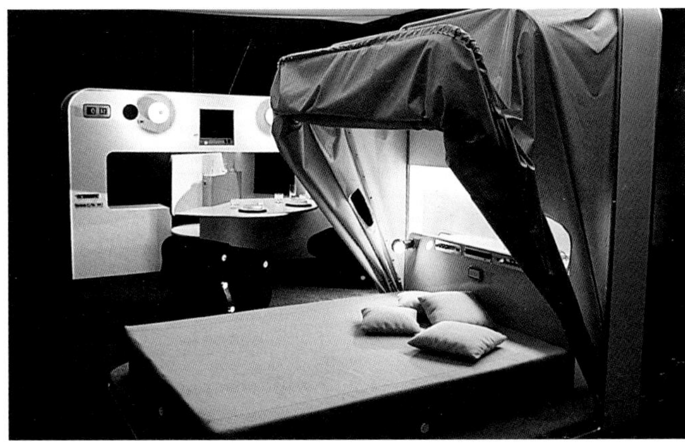

bathroom, storage, and sleeping arrangements of the complete system. In the text accompanying the exhibition, Colombo stipulated: "The space within this unit should be dynamic, that is, it should be in a continual state of transformation, so that a cubic space smaller than the norm can nevertheless be exploited to the maximum economy in its interior arrangement." The home of the future, according to Colombo, was not a series of static rooms designed around specific functions, but a dynamic, open space where furniture and appliances were transformed to best suit the activity to be undertaken. He expressed a belief that "the dwelling should be adapted more and more to man, rather than the other way around," an opinion shared by many designers and architects at the time.

The major difference between Colombo's earlier living systems and the *Total Furnishing Unit* he designed for MoMA, is the decline in prominence of the bed. In the design of the *Habitation Capsule* exhibited at Visiona 1, the bed is the prime focus of the whole arrangement. It is a large and inviting area of recreation, complete with its own entertainment

Top left: Joe Colombo, *Cabriolet-Bed*, Sormani, 1969.

Top right: Joe Colombo, *Total Furnishing Unit*, 1971. The two single beds are hidden away beneath the shelving unit.

Left: Joe Colombo, *Tube* chair, Flexform, 1969.

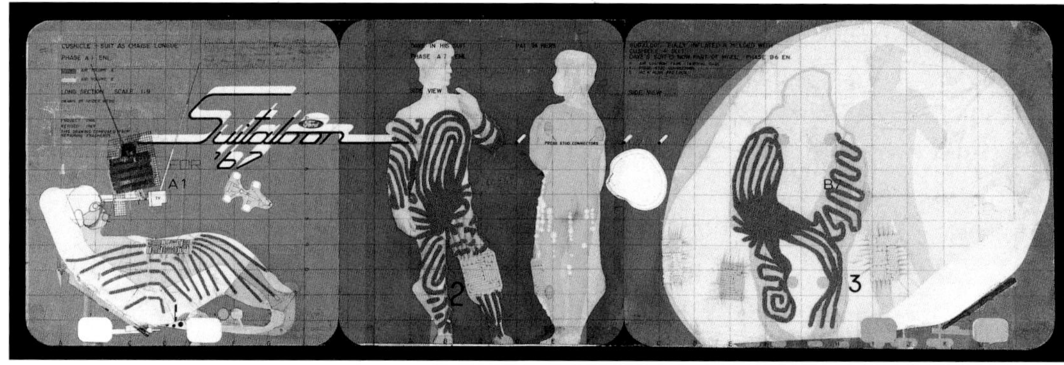

Top: Michael Webb, *Suitaloon '67*, 1966–69.

system. *Cabriolet-Bed*, too, is similar in that it became the main attraction of the space. In *Total Furnishing Unit*, the bed was split into two separated berths, which were hidden away when not in use. The system gave work greater priority over play and the positioning of the beds implied they were used solely for rest and recuperation, rather than recreation. The earlier living units suggested an abundance of leisure time and casual sex as an entertaining diversion. However, as reflected in the spartan functionality of *Total Furnishing Unit*, the buoyant, fun-loving mood often associated with the 1960s and the height of the space race was on the decline.

The first citizens of the space age were on the move. Home-owners moved house more and more regularly and the demand for rental accommodation increased dramatically. The new throwaway culture, where a person's relationship to his possessions was forever shortening, took effect in the housing market. Workers in the new electronics and space industries were particularly noted for their propensity to relocate. It was an in-house joke at computer giant IBM that the firm's initials really stood for "I've been moved". The boom in rental accommodation was partly credited to a desire for "minimum involvement housing," a concept that added the house to the growing list of short-term commodities. This was further indication that the home—the basic component of any society—was undergoing a revolution.

Since the early 1960s, the London-based group, Archigram, comprising of architects Warren Chalk, Peter Cook, Dennis Crompton, David Greene, Ron Herron, and Michael Webb, had been calling for buildings that could be regarded as expendable consumer goods. The third issue of the Archigram publication was subtitled "Towards a Throwaway Architecture" and on the pages inside, the home and the whole city were likened to a disposable pack of frozen peas. The throwaway society and all the moving from place to place inspired a new trend for a temporary, placeless architecture. For Archigram, this resulted in projects such as *Blow-out Village* (1966) and *Walking City* (1964). Both projects were inspired by motion and flexibility. *Blow-out Village* transformed, through a series of hydraulic pumps and telescopic arms, from a small package on a hovercraft-type base to a collection of homes beneath a transparent dome. *Walking City* was a beast: hefty telescopic legs did the walking and its belly was stuffed with row upon row of apartments, together with all the facilities one would expect to find in a teeming metropolis.

In his essay *A Necessary Irritant*, Barry Curtis describes how "new technology challenged architecture because it promised constant change, new experiences and a high degree of self-

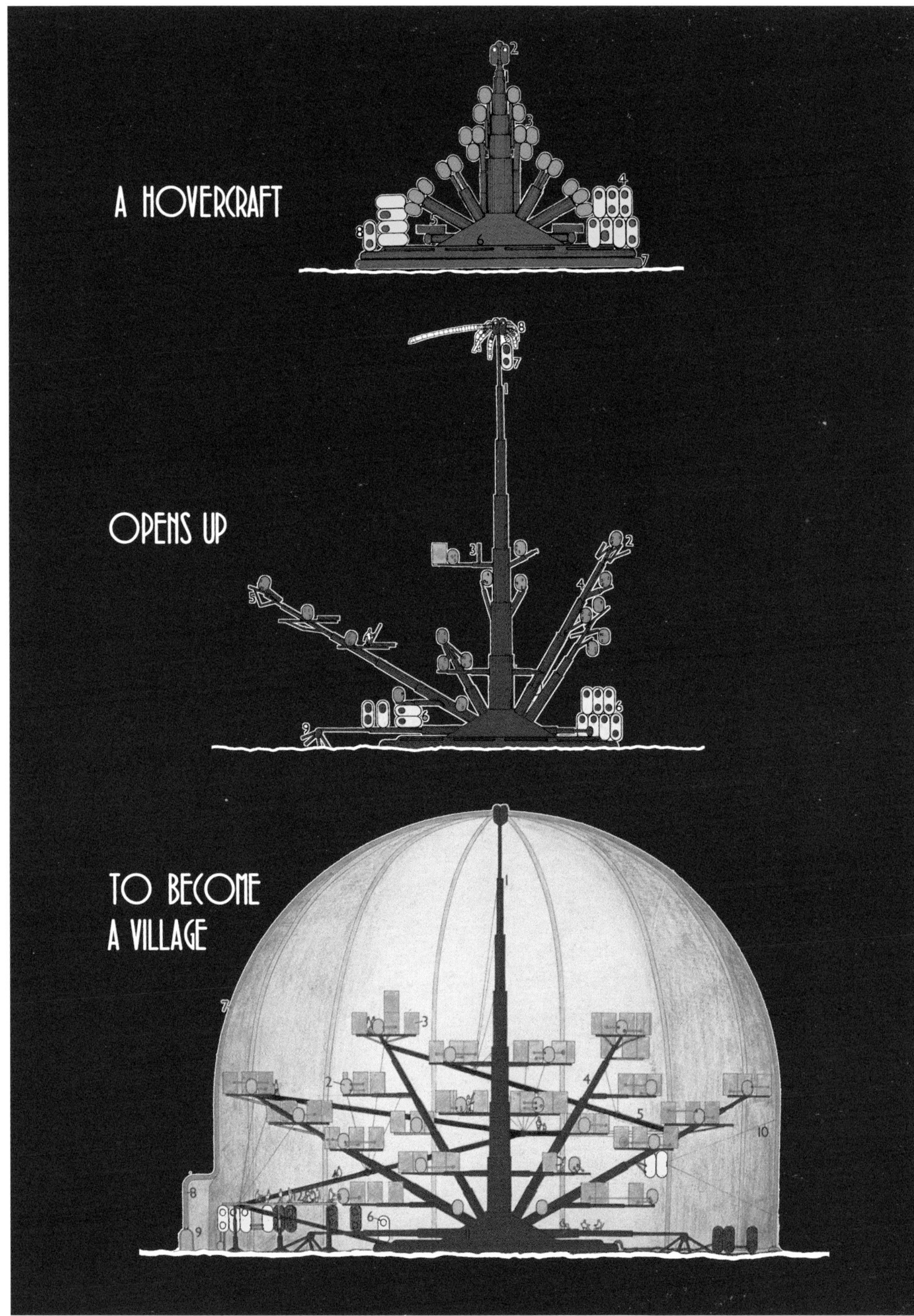

Left: Peter Cook, *Blow-Out Village*, 1966.

sufficiency and independence for the intelligent consumer." The Archigram group responded to this challenge and integrated the latest space-age technology into their plans and schemes for flexible dwellings, one of the most notable being the heavily automated *1990 House* (1967). Here robots, domestic appliances, furniture and transportation were all fused together to create an environment where the inhabitants could change and adapt the living arrangements to best suit to their needs. The individual apartments plugged into a megastructure, which provided all the essential services such as energy, water, and sanitation.

Top: Warren Chalk, Peter Cook, Dennis Crompton, Ron Herron, *1990 House*, 1967.

Other Archigram projects, such as *Cushicle* (1966) and *Suitaloon* (1966–69), were tiny in comparison to the megastructure of *1990 House* or the gargantuan *Walking City*, however, their impact was just as impressive. In these proposals, a body suit could be expanded to form an inflated shelter with room enough for two. Archigram envisaged a new breed of nomads who carried their homes with them, just like an astronaut encapsulated in the

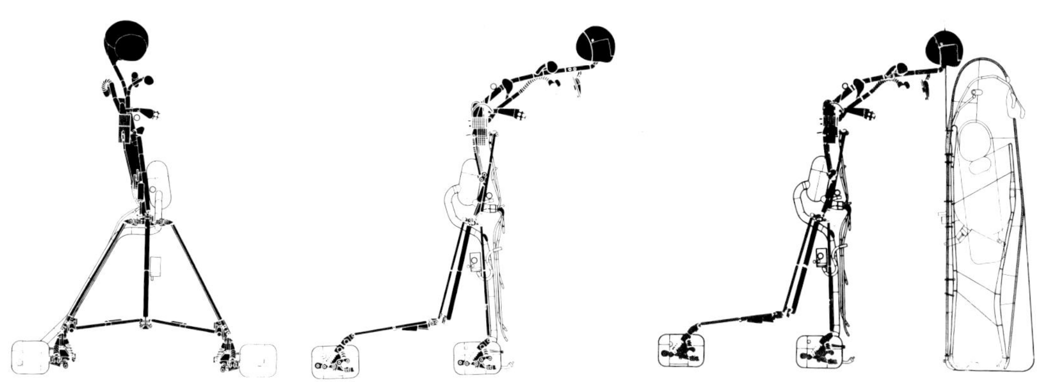

protective environment of his EVA suit. Positioned somewhere in between *1990 House* and *Suitaloon* is the high-tech capsule, *Living Pod* (1966), designed by Archigram's David Greene. The sculpted exterior of this futuristic habitation unit resembled the Apollo Lunar Module and the interior featured all manner of automated gadgets. It was just one of many designs of this era where the organization of living space was similar to the inside of a space station. There were no rooms as such—the interior space was transformed through different states by pneumatic partitions and flexible furniture. The essential facilities for washing and waste disposal were clipped on to the upper deck of the capsule and protruded from its exterior. Compact and flexible, *Living Pod* challenged the old conception of the home, and also its traditional inhabitants, the nuclear family.

Neatly encapsulated units similar to *Living Pod* became the focus of attention for numerous architects at the onset of the space age. As early as 1962, the Japanese philosopher and architect, Kisho Kurokawa, began experimenting with designs for modular

Top: Michael Webb and David Greene, full-size model of the *Cushicle* with David Greene inside, 1966.

Above left: Michael Webb and David Greene, *Suitaloon*, 1968.

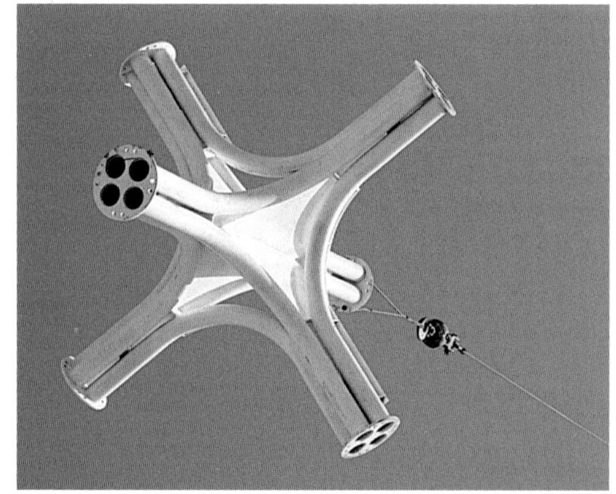

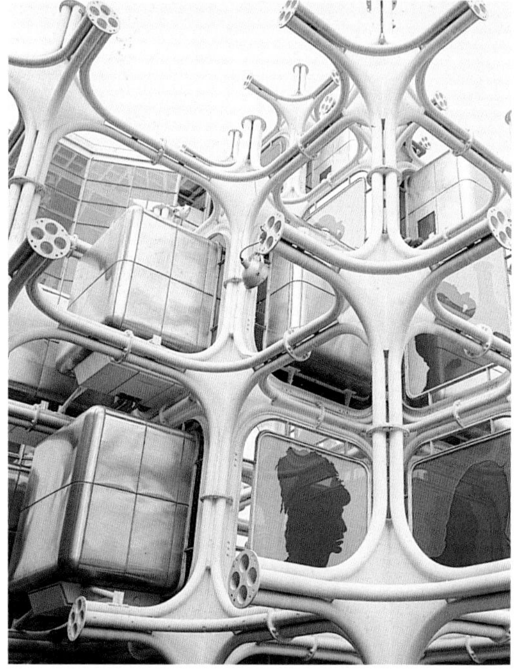

Top:
Kisho Kurokawa, *Takara Beautilion*, design 1968, construction 1969. Steel pipes bent to an angle of 90 degrees were welded to steel plates to create the structure's modular framework.

dwellings. Kurokawa was a prominent figure in the Metabolist movement, a group of architects who designed adaptable buildings capable of continuous transformation through expansion and contraction. Their approach was inspired by life and biological processes rather than machines and heavy industry. In an interview in 1997, Kurokawa commented on the philosophy behind Metabolism: "How can we control technology and at the same time avoid technology controlling us? To me Metabolism is the idea of finding methods for controlling technology." His words echo similar concerns to those expressed by other architects of the time, such as Archigram and the Austrian collectives Coop Himmelb(l)au and Haus-Rucker-Co, who felt that the built environment was becoming too formal and machine-like.

Kurokawa designed a prototype plug-in mega-structure at the Osaka Expo of 1970 as a pavilion for the Takara corporation. Standing outside the pavilion were a cluster of white, sentinel-like

Left:
Kisho Kurokawa, *Takara Beautilion*, design 1968, construction 1969. The building is a classic example of Metabolist architecture and was dismantled after six months' service at Expo '70, Osaka.

Top:
Kisho Kurokawa, *Nakagin Capsule Tower*, Tokyo, Japan, design 1970, construction 1971–72. When the residential district of Tokyo began shifting to the suburbs, this building was conceived to bring housing units back to the city center.

towers. They resembled the discharged stages of a rocket and rings of lamps, arranged around their bases like small boosters, added to this effect. Convex mirrors, similar to the reflective visor fronting an astronaut's headpiece, were positioned like faces at the top of each tower. The pavilion itself, named the Takara Beautilion, was constructed around a framework of prefabricated components made from curved steel piping. It looked like a giant erector set and had its tubular skeleton on full show like scaffolding around a construction site. The framework also possessed the flexibility and impermanence of scaffolding in that it could be erected and dismantled with relative ease. When fastened together, the segments of steel piping formed a chassis of cubic spaces and inserted into several of these spaces were Kurokawa's Living Capsules. Each self-contained unit had its own kitchen, bathroom, living, and sleeping areas, and also a lavish dressing room. In some cases the capsules were fluffy and had fur-like carpet covering the floor, walls and ceiling, which was a

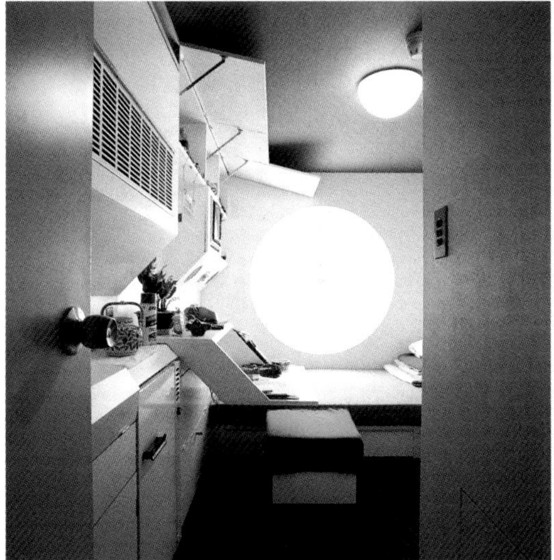

little impractical for the kitchen. However, the concept brought a more flexible approach to high-density housing and sought to address the dilemma that mass production automatically resulted in uniformity. The overall appearance of the Takara Beautilion, with its informal pattern of tubes, capsules, and vacant spaces, certainly dispensed with the image of manufactured uniformity.

Kurokawa finally realized his concept of a plug-in megastructure in the Nakagin Capsule Tower, Tokyo, which was completed in 1972. Here, concrete replaced steel in the provision of the building's framework and its facilities' core. The individual capsules could be added and removed as and when required. The floor space of the units measured only 2.4 x 3.6 meters, yet each comprised its own bathroom, kitchen, storage, living and sleeping areas. The individual capsules were conceived to cater for a single occupant but numerous units could be joined together to cater for a couple or family. The Nakagin Capsule Tower realizes some of Kurokawa's key philosophies. Each unit can be exchanged and

Above:
Kisho Kurokawa, *Nakagin Capsule Tower*, Tokyo, Japan, design 1970, construction 1971–1972. The apartments are compact and provide Tokyo's commuters with a studio, a place to sleep, or a space for social activities.

recycled and therefore made the whole structure sustainable. The core structure was built to last, but the units were transient, and the capsules represent a totally integrated system for living. The condensed lifestyle each multi-purpose container afforded was like that of an encapsulated astronaut traveling through outer space. Furniture and appliances were compact and could be stowed away when not in use. The capsule transformed between states; its arrangement was dynamic and ever-changing, and everything was controlled by the actions of its inhabitant.

The Osaka '70 Expo was an overwhelming celebration of new technology, the space age, and the future. Mammoth inflatable buildings and all manner of futuristic pavilions towered over the festival site, which was patrolled by various robots and automated appliances. The fair's central theme was "Progress and Harmony for Mankind", however, there were already signs that the future would not be as progressive or as harmonious as the exhibitors implied. Volatile demonstrations, including nude marches, were held in protest at the overblown commercialism of the event. Security was stepped up at the United States' pavilion, which housed a chunk of moon rock, for fear of attacks from anti-Vietnam war protesters. In other respects, however, this fair was an accurate portrayal of what was to come. Many of the pavilions fabricated by individual companies dwarfed those erected by whole nations, a move that foreshadowed the dramatic rise in power and wealth of the global corporations.

Osaka '70 was the first Expo event to be held in Asia and was intended to be a significant break from all the world's fairs of the past. Its chief planners, the architects Kenzo Tange, Arata Isozaki, and Yoshiaki Tono, wanted to create an environment where the public could interact with advanced technology. According to Isozaki, the Expo was going to initiate "a new century of design and planning and visitor participation—the first 'post-industrial' exposition." The arrival of the post-industrial era saw software (information and programming with no physical presence) take precedence over hardware (machines and products with physical dimensions). Communication was the basis of the new age and manufactured products began losing out to information and services. Expo '70 was to reflect this shift in the economy. However, the software-led desires of the planners came into conflict with the hardware concerns of certain exhibitors and the result was a chaotic mishmash of everything.

The arrival of the space age was also making its presence felt in the work of avant-garde architects and counter-culture groups across Japan, Europe, and the USA. Concern about the growing incompatibility between the individual and architecture was expressed in America by Chip Lord, Doug Michels, and Curtis Schreier, known

collectively as Ant Farm. This group rejected the industrial city and created temporary shelters, with names such as Dreamcloud and Flagbag, to house concerts, conferences and happenings in the American deserts. In 1969, these "space cowboys" staged a series of total experience environments across Texas and created "electronic oases" to nourish the minds of new "media nomads." The following year they published the *Inflatocookbook* as a way of sharing their expertise in the construction of inflatable shelters. Ant Farm embraced the spirit of the space age and combined new technology with a DIY mentality in the creation of a force intended to liberate citizens from the order of the city.

In Austria, the Vienna-based collectives Haus-Rucker-Co and Coop Himmelb(l)au captured a mood of rebellion against the architecture of the day, which was considered to be homogeneous and dehumanizing. The social housing projects of the post-war years, which shot-up across cities such as Vienna in the 1950s and 1960s, came to represent an increasingly harsh environment. The repetitive arrangement of these concrete boxes evoked a scenario of humans who were slaves to the machine.

This new generation of architects devised a softer, more individual-oriented future with structures far removed from the monotonous buildings looming over their city. Rather than forcing inhabitants to fit their lives into a standardized dwelling these architects proposed structures that responded to human actions and emotions. Inspired by the likes of Walter Pichler, Hans Hollein and Archigram, Haus-Rucker-Co and Coop Himmelb(l)au set about rehumanizing the environment with their designs for "cities that fly like breath."

Inflatable technology provided the perfect means for both Coop Himmelb(l)au and Haus-Rucker-Co to put their ideas into practice. These groups did not want to erect huge stone monuments that would be around for hundreds of years. They called instead for

Top: To celebrate America's recent conquest of the moon a lunar theme was adopted in its pavilion at Expo '70 in Osaka, Japan.

Top: Coop Himmelb(l)au, *Villa Rosa*, 1968. The large inflated sphere is a relaxation chamber and the space leading into it can be transformed via the inflation and deflation of the surrounding balloons.

an architecture more in keeping with the time; an architecture that was transient, flexible and even disposable, but also, an architecture that was ergonomic and responsive to the needs of the people using it. Coop Himmelb(l)au, founded in 1968 by Wolf D. Prix, Helmut Swiczinsky and Rainer Michael Holzer, made their philosophy clear: "We should not have to change in order to live within architecture, but architecture has to react to our movements, feelings, moods, emotions, so that we want to live within it." Their words echoed Joe Colombo's statement that "the dwelling should be adapted more and more to man", and their approach resulted in the construction and testing of a dwelling named Villa Rosa (1968). This prototype comprised of three cells including an inflatable relaxation chamber complete with revolving bed; a transformable space determined by the inflation and deflation of eight balloons; and a detachable, portable shelter. Villa Rosa took the notion of lounging to the extreme and a piped-in sequence of visual, acoustic, and aromatic sensations transformed the mood even further.

Haus-Rucker-Co, comprising the architects Laudris Ortner, Günter Zamp Kelp, and Klaus Pinter, developed a similar unit to Villa Rosa called *Gelbes Herz* (1968). The device consisted of a pulsating bubble inside a large inflatable capsule, which was supported by a waist-high metal frame. At its core was a bed with ample room for two people to recline and take it easy. A repeat pattern of inflation and deflation created a soft, pulsating rhythm, to which the inhabitants were supposed to adapt and relax. They also initiated the concept of Vanilla Future with the statement: "For many people the future is scary.

Left:
Coop Himmelb(l)au, *Astroballon*, 1969. The sound of the wearer's heartbeat is amplified through speakers and also transformed into a pulsating light sequence.

Full of horrible robots and strange rays. For us the future is bright yellow like vanilla ice cream. Refreshing, smelling nice and soft. Vanilla Future."

Gelbes Herz was part of a whole range of projects under the umbrella of the Mind Expanding Program. Other devices included a collection of bizarre helmets with colored visors, flashing lights and stereo earphones. These plastic headpieces, with the names *Flyhead*, *Viewatomizer*, *Drizzler*, and *Environment Transformer* (all 1968), were said to isolate the wearer from the outside world. The helmets placed a buffer between the real world and the senses of the person inside. *Mind-Expander I* (1967) and *Mind-Expander II* (1968/69) were similar to the helmets, only much bigger and with an intimate seating arrangement for two. They featured an electronic display of light and sound, which was intended to induce a trance-like state similar to that reached through mind-bending drugs or a shamanic ritual. Haus-Rucker-Co also embraced the space age

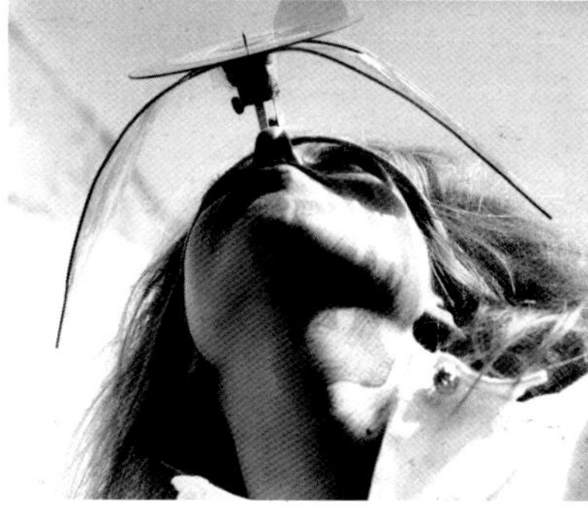

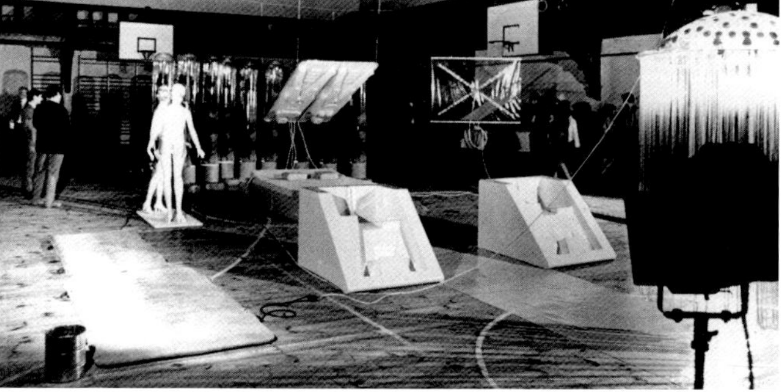

Top left:
Haus-Rucker-Co, *Mind Expander I*, 1967.

Top right:
Haus-Rucker-Co, *Electric Skin*.

Bottom left:
Haus-Rucker-Co, *Drizzler*, 1968.

Bottom right:
Interior view of *Vanilla Future*, an exhibition mounted by Haus-Rucker-Co at the Kraftsporthalle, Schleifmühlgasse, Vienna, Austria, 1969.

Left: Haus-Rucker-Co, *Fly Head*, 1968.

Right: Haus-Rucker-Co, *Mind Expander II*, 1968–69.

in other ventures. In *Mondessen* (1969) they celebrated the Apollo lunar landing by dressing up as astronauts and handing out slices of a huge moon-shaped cake covered with marzipan craters to the Viennese public, in an echo of the 1962 celebrations on Cocoa Beach, USA.

Haus-Rucker-Co and Coop Himmelb(l)au blended space-age technology, striking visuals, and unusual sounds in their efforts to create an environment that worked in harmony with its inhabitants. Through the use of inflatable chambers that moved and breathed they fused architecture with the mechanics of the human body. Both groups called for a more fluid and responsive approach to construction. They placed the experience of a building above its physical appearance and called for a flexible future where people are in full control of their surroundings.

Ant Farm, Coop-Himmelb(l)au, and Haus-Rucker-Co exploited inflatable technology to a radical extreme, but air-filled forms also infiltrated a more conventional arena. The extensive application of pneumatic devices in outer space, as used in the Telstar communications satellite, prototype lunar bases, and numerous EVA suits, inspired the creation of a whole flotilla of inflatable commodities for the home. Paris-based architect Nguyen Manh Khanh, husband of fashion designer Emmanuelle Khanh, designed a range of inflatable furniture through his firm Quasar.

Quasar's *Suspension Aérospace* lamp (1967) uses inflation as a means of transformation from a flat piece of plastic to swollen blob in a matter of seconds. This glowing sack of air could be suspended from the ceiling and its puffed-up, ellipsoid shape gave it an other-worldly presence. The various seating elements made by Quasar enjoyed space-age names such as *Satellite*, *Moonport*, and *Apollo*. However, Khanh also fabricated pneumatic partitions, a chaise longue, a coffee table, and even an inflatable house to arrange them all in. Quasar's cylindrical house was made entirely of inflatable PVC. A fat air-filled ring at the base of the structure and a slightly thinner ring around the top held a series of pneumatic wall panels in place. These panels were fastened together and anchored to the two holding rings by a series of chains and mooring hooks. An inflated dome capped the structure and an inflatable floor could be added to enable the house to float on water. The whole ensemble was transparent, which gives it the appearance of weightlessness—another space-age attribute.

Paris witnessed an explosion of inflatable furniture and architecture in the late 1960s. The Utopie group of architects, which comprised Jean Aubert, Jean Paul Jungmann and Antoine Stinco among others, celebrated the inflatable form in an exhibition entitled *Structures Gonflables* in Paris, March 1968. On

display were all kinds of pneumatic devices including their own range of blow-up furniture manufactured under the company name AJS Aerolande. Like Quasar's wall panels, AJS Aerolande's furniture was modular and could be rearranged to form seating, partition or sleeping elements. Their *Tore* chair had a flocked coating so the sticky PVC did not come into contact with a person's skin once they were seated. The flexibility of AJS Aerolande's furniture and the group's attention to detail make it one of the most successful examples of the era.

Inflatable furniture was thought to be particularly appealing to those living in small, cramped apartments. An article in the Weekend *Telegraph* Magazine of November 1967 referred to those residing in such dwellings as the "no-space generation" and cited inflatable chairs as their savior. Others announced the new craze for pneumatic furniture as "a revolution in our domestic mores" and that "these unusual blow-up pieces are going to affect the design of furniture in a decisive kind of way." Needless to say, it did not. The craze was a short-lived fad and all but disappeared by the early 1970s. However, inflatable furniture demonstrates, yet again, that the ideal home of the space age was a playful and relaxed environment. Like the globular plastic chairs of Eero Aarnio, air-filled furniture exploited advanced technology to bring unusual forms into the home. The seating modules produced by Quasar and AJS Aerolande are the perfect, youthful response to the hard industrial furniture made popular by the Modern movement.

Another designer to experiment with designs for air-filled furniture was Verner Panton, who created a series of inflatable cubes for the Plus-Linje furniture company in 1961. By themselves, these modules performed as a chair or footstool, but, they could be fitted together to make a sofa or bed. It was the introduction of high frequency PVC welding at this time that made inflatable furniture a realistic proposition for the home. This innovation made it possible to join sheets of PVC together with a thin

Top: Quasar Khanh (Nguyen Manh Khanh), *Suspension Aérospace* lamp, France, 1967.

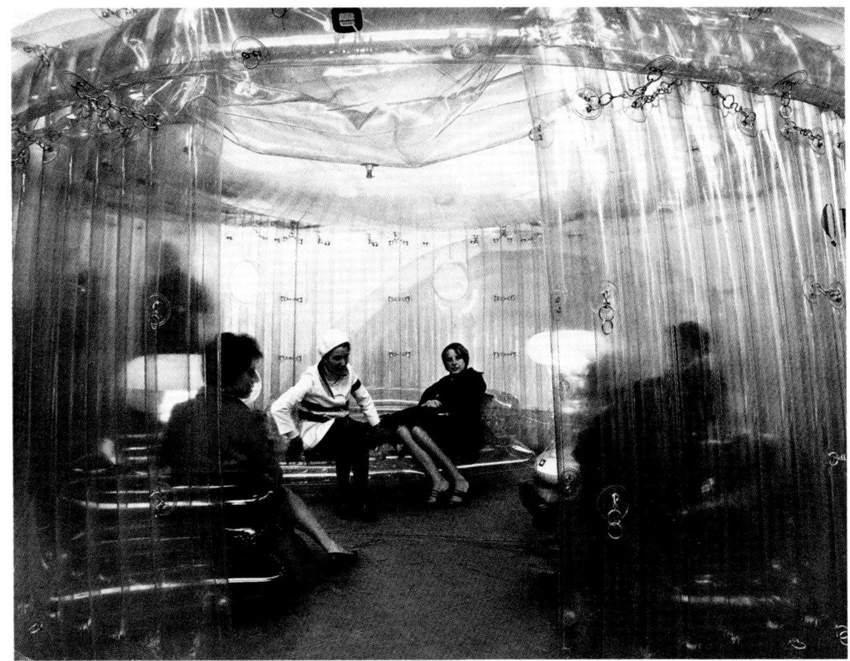

Left: Interior view of *Structures Gonflables*, an exhibition mounted by the Utopie group at the Musée d'Art Moderne de la Ville de Paris–ARC, March 1–30, 1968. Furniture and cylindrical house by Quasar Khanh (Nguyen Manh Khanh), 1967.

Center left and right: AJS Aerolande (Jean Aubert, Jean Paul Jungmann and Antoine Stinco), *Tore* armchair, manufactured by Kléber Renolit Plastiques, France, 1967.

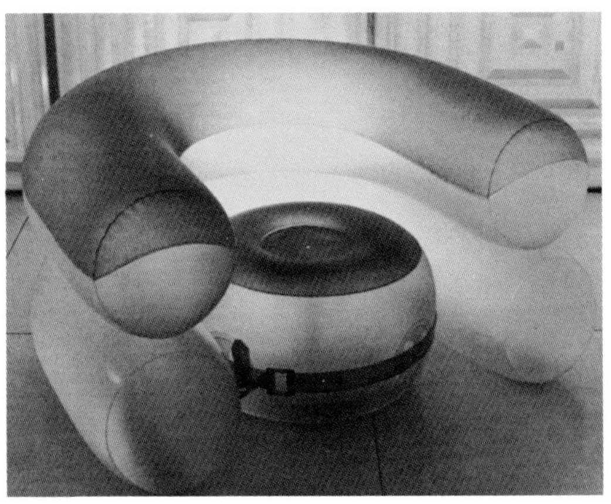

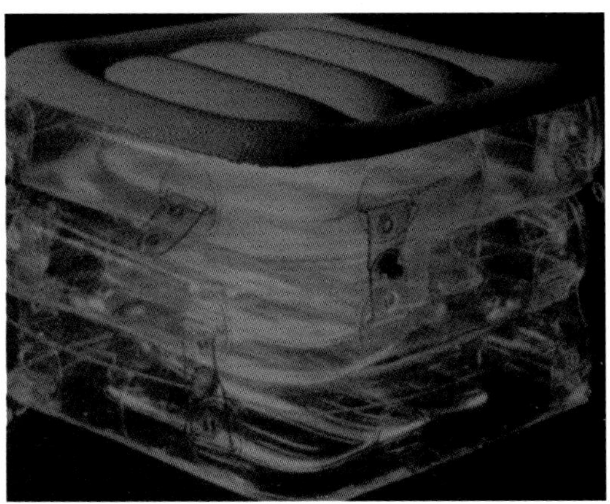

Far left: AJS Aerolande (Jean Aubert, Jean Paul Jungmann and Antoine Stinco), *Carré* cushion, manufactured by Kléber Renolit Plastiques, France,1967.

Left: Verner Panton, *Inflatable Module*, manufactured by Plus-Linje, Mobilia 73/1961.

and air-tight seam. Moreover, it enabled a new generation of consumers to bring a slice of the space age into their own homes.

Air-filled furniture attempted to lighten up the domestic interior, but this was achieved with greater success by the new chemically manufactured foams. Verner Panton confirmed his position as a grand master of 20th century design with the iconic *Panton* chair in 1968. His work is characterized by intensive research into synthetic materials and high-tech manufacturing processes. Both Danish architect Arne Jacobsen, whom Panton assisted for a brief period in the early 1950s, and designer Pøul Henningsen, who taught Panton at Copenhagen's Royal Academy of Art, had enormous influence on his methodical approach and fascination for new materials.

The futuristic lamps, *Moon* (1960), *Flower Pot* (1968), and *VP Globe* (1970), all manufactured by Louis Poulsen, demonstrate Panton's passion for the space-age style. *Moon* plays with the eclipse effect and consists of white, circular bands arranged around a single light source. *Flower Pot* resembles a simple flying saucer and *VP Globe* a complex satellite. Panton's *Easy Chair C1* (1959), manufactured by Plus-Linje, has a hemispherical seat and slender chrome-plated leg and appears to defy gravity in typical space-age style. However, Panton

Top: Verner Panton, *VP Globe* suspended lamp, manufactured by Louis Poulsen, 1970.

did much more than apply a futuristic aesthetic to household products. He unified whole interior spaces by removing the divisions between walls, floor and ceiling, and reshaped the domestic landscape as a space for chatting and chilling out.

"A departure from traditional living" was the theme of the futuristic interior created by Panton for the Bayer chemical corporation at the Cologne Furniture Fair of 1968. Panton was handed the task of designing an environment that would demonstrate the versatility of Bayer's man-made fibers and he became the first in a series of designers to do so. The Dralon Boat was the exhibition space allocated to Panton and he completely abandoned the traditional domestic interior in favor of his own playful meanderings on the home of the future. In opposition to the functionality of Joe Colombo's later furnishing units exhibited the following year, Verner Panton envisaged the future home as a space dedicated to relaxation. His vision included none of the multi-purpose machines or space-saving kitchen appliances associated with condensed living. "Cooking will become a hobby," predicted Panton in a 1967 interview in *Stern* magazine, "entire menus come out of the food factory ready to eat." He went on to suggest that by the year 2000, "housework as we know it will not exist." He was

Top: Verner Panton, *Flower Pot* suspended lamp, manufactured by Louis Poulsen, 1968.

Top: Interior view of Verner Panton's installation at *Visiona 0: A Departure from Traditional Living*, Dralon Boat, Cologne Furniture Fair, 1968. It includes Panton's *Flying Chairs*, 1964 and Pøul Henningsen's *Artichoke* suspended lamp, 1959.

way off the mark, but that does not matter. In retrospect, it is the belief that the home would change in such a radical fashion that today seems so remarkable. The confidence demonstrated by designers such as Panton and Colombo in their visions of the future demonstrate the passions inspired by the space age.

Panton applied his unique approach to the whole of the Dralon Boat and created an extraordinarily tactile environment. His *Flying Chairs* (1964) were suspended from the ceiling of one room and a corridor was furnished with large foam balls, coated in a fleece-like fabric that matched the carpet. It was a free arrangement of soft, casual seating that, according to Sabine Epple, in the book *Verner Panton: The Collected Works*, "generated an atmosphere of well-being and ease." Sculpted foam blocks, with spaces cut away for reclining and sitting, filled spaces from floor to ceiling in one of the rooms, and on the upper deck he unveiled a new affordable seating system aimed at the mass market. This system consisted of geometrically shaped modules of foam, which interlocked in different patterns and enabled consumers to rethink and reshape the layout of their own house. The foam segments were like a grown-up version of a child's set of building blocks and invited playful experimentation into the home.

Synthetic foams, like air-filled PVC, provided a means of softening the domestic interior. The unique qualities of this material were embraced by a number of designers, who exploited it to create unusual and futuristic forms. The structural properties of the higher density foams, such as

Left: Interior view of Verner Panton's installation at *Visiona 0: A Departure from Traditional Living*, Dralon Boat, Cologne Furniture Fair, 1968. It includes Panton's *Furry Ball* seat units, 1968.

Top: Pierre Paulin, *Tongue* (No F582) armchair, manufactured by Artifort, Netherlands, 1967.

those used by Panton in the Dralon Boat, meant that large pieces of furniture could be manufactured without the need for a rigid supporting framework. Panton's Upholstered Seating System of 1963, demonstrates a more common use for foam. In this series of chairs it is used as a soft and comfortable coating over a hard internal frame. None of the sliver-like frame is exposed only the upholstery, which softens its overall appearance. French designers Olivier Mourgue and Pierre Paulin were particularly noted for their expertise in combining cushioned surfaces with solid internal structures. Mourgue's *Djinn* chair and stool (1965), and Paulin's *Tongue* (1967) and *Ribbon* (1965) armchairs, all manufactured by Artifort, are exemplary demonstrations of the free-flowing forms that can be created via this technique.

Bayer again invited Panton to shape the interior of the Dralon Boat in 1970, on the event of Visiona 2, the theme of which was, the "Question of Living Tomorrow." Joe Colombo had addressed this notion the previous year with his futuristic *Habitation Capsule*, which made extensive use of Bayer's synthetic plastics. Now Panton was to have a second shot and he transformed the Dralon Boat into an orgy of bright colors and futuristic forms. The Visiona events handed Panton, Colombo, and in 1971, Olivier Mourgue, a rare opportunity to project their

Top: Verner Panton, *Studioline*, upholstered furniture system, 1961; Bar furniture *Barboy*, 1963; *Topan* pendant lamp, 1959.

Left: Pierre Paulin, *Ribbon* (No F582) armchair, manufactured by Artifort, Netherlands, 1965.

Right: Interior view of Verner Panton's *Green Room* installation at *Visiona 2: A Question of Living Tomorrow,* Dralon Boat, Cologne Furniture Fair, 1970.

Left: Verner Panton, *Swimming Pool*, Spiegel Publishing House, Hamburg, Germany, 1969.

Top:
Verner Panton
Visiona 2, Cologne Furniture Fair, 1970.
Mushroom lamp, 1969, Bayer;
Soft Line, 1969, Herman Miller/Fehlbaum;
Round cupboard, 1969, Bayer.

ideas with the utmost freedom and finance to match. The designers built a bridge of communication between the manufacturer and the consumer. Their work furnished an exciting realm where visitors were able to experience the very latest materials and technologies in a fashion rarely witnessed on such a complete scale. In *Verner Panton: The Collected Works*, Sabine Epple emphasizes the unique opportunity offered by the event, when she says, "No other form of exhibition offered designers such optimum conditions ...One would be justified in speaking, without exaggeration, of one of the greatest moments in the collaboration between design and industry."

The traditional home was left even further behind in the installation for Visiona 2. "The function of apartments in the future," suggested Panton in 1970, "will change to the effect that people will be able to use them to recover from the daily pressure to do well and achieve results." To that end, the whole Dralon Boat was converted into a luxurious calm-inducing retreat. Color was used to

unify each zone as Panton presented spaces where everything—from carpet to seating to ceiling—was red or green or purple. The space-age styling evolved into the creation of an inner space with internal organs. The most expressive use of color and form appeared in his *Phantasy Landscape*, a psychedelic maze of tunnels, chambers, and interconnecting cavities. This centerpiece of the exhibition was an extreme incarnation of the modular foam interior landscape presented in 1968. The arrangement of different shapes was remarkable but it was the exuberant use of color that dominated the whole scenario. The concentration of warm colors in the center of the organic terrain gave rise to a glowing effect amid the cool colors surrounding it. Far removed from the clean, automated interiors inspired by spacecraft it projected a futuristic inner reality of individualism and self-indulgence.

The visions of the future presented by Verner Panton and Joe Colombo at the Cologne Furniture Fair emphasize recreation and site the bed at the

Top: Verner Panton, *Mirror Collection*, small series, 1965. A mirrored wall covering made up of square and triangular modules.

core of the home. In Panton's vision there are no household chores to undertake, in Colombo's they are made easy by automation. Home can be found in the city and provides a sanctuary from the hustle and bustle of urban life. The atmosphere is seductive and charged with eroticism. It was a sharp contrast to the ideal home of the previous era.

The bright, popular modern home portrayed in so many commercials of the early 1950s was a suburban hive of activity and often flooded with daylight. It was all effectively managed by a cheerful, wavy-haired housewife from the kitchen—a working room where the whole family was nourished. The space-age home is dimly lit by pools of artificial light: it is not a family home but a bachelor pad or sex den for young couples. The bed is the focus—a place of relaxation and sexual nourishment. In the space age, the idealized image of domestic bliss was subverted from a wholesome family home into a high-tech pleasure capsule.

Design in the space age was a celebration of youth and vitality, but with youth comes irresponsibility. The ideal home of this period reflects a society aspiring to a life of zero responsibility, where everyday tasks are automated and all products are disposable. In the years immediately after World War II, design responded to a desire among consumers for a steady job and the stability of family life. In the years of the space age, design fed to a desire to lounge around and have casual sex while machines did all the work.

Those first years in space saw many changes taking place on the earth. The foundation of the industrialized world began to shift from a manufacturing base to one of services and information. Futuristic design embraced this change and looked forward with optimism rather than fear; but it all happened too fast and very few were ready to leave the past behind. The excitement generated by space travel had made pondering the future a fashionable occupation. In hindsight, it is easy to say that many of the visions of the future were naive, or even ridiculous—but this is exactly why the era now seems so refreshing. There would have been little point in designers envisaging a future where everything in it remained pretty much the same except that the lapels grew wider and the people wore flares.

The space-age look was slick and seductive, but the backlash soon came. The futuristic style was rejected in favor of a return to the hand-crafted look. Synthetic materials were deemed cheap and nasty. All the boasts of conquering nature were now frowned upon as the era characterized by its obsession with youth was forced to grow up. The throwaway society was causing an environmental catastrophe and the "Question of Living Tomorrow" took on a new, and fearful meaning.

Left: Verner Panton, *Phantasy Landscape* installation at *Visiona 2: A Question of Living Tomorrow*, Cologne Furniture Fair, 1970.

Right: Andrew Grassie, *Fir Tree Hinterland*, 1999, (detail).
Oil on canvas, 60 x 75 cm.

03 "We came in peace for all mankind"

By the time Johnny Rotten screamed "No future" on the Sex Pistols's 1977 single, *God Save the Queen* any notion of a space-age Utopia had been laid to rest. In just a few short years, the child-like optimism that had characterized the 1960s had been annihilated. Its demise was accelerated by the oil crisis of 1973 and the global recession that followed. Three decades on and our feelings about the conquest of space and the visions it inspired are as mixed as ever.

It is unlikely that space travel will ever generate the sort of frenzy it did in the 1960s. The period after the Apollo moon landings saw the scientific exploitation of space take precedence over the public spectacle. However, the European Space Agency (ESA) recently enlisted well-known artists in an attempt to bring space exploration back into the public arena.

The Beagle 2 probe, designed by scientist Colin Pillinger, is part of the ESA's Mars Express mission. It is due to launch in summer 2003 and will touch down on the red planet to analyze rock samples for signs of life. The Martian probe is a UK-led project and because space research does not have a high priority in Britain, Pillinger looked into alternative ways of generating interest in the mission. Help for the scientific expedition was found in the unlikely guise of musicians from the rock group Blur and artist Damien Hirst. Blur composed a track based on a mathematical sequence to act as a call sign once the Beagle has landed. A spot painting by Damien Hirst will be used as an instrument calibration chart to check everything is in order after touchdown. Hirst's painting was created with special pigments that are tough enough to withstand the extremities of the Martian environment. Beagle 2 has gained much wider attention than usual because of the artwork it will carry, and thus Pillinger has successfully combined art and science to promote the project and help deliver space exploration to a broader public.

The arrival of space tourism has also helped to restore activity in space to a wider audience. While the notion of colonizing the moon or Mars has long been forgotten, the possibility of taking a holiday in space finally happened on April 28, 2001. Californian businessman Dennis Tito paid $20 million for a trip on a Russian supply ship to the International Space Station (ISS). The flight realized a boyhood ambition for the 60-year-old former space scientist, who had designed flight trajectories for three proposed NASA missions to Mars in the 1960s. The pioneering trip was not without controversy. Tito had to sign a contract freeing all national space agencies of responsibility in the event of an accident. He also had to agree to pay for any damage he caused while on the space station and was banned by NASA from entering the United

Top: Charles Luckman, William Pereira, Welton Becket, and Paul R. Williams, Theme Building, Los Angeles International Airport, Los Angeles, USA, 1962, exterior illumination designed by Michael Valentino, Walt Disney Imagineering, 1997.

States' zones of the ISS without an escort. Tito was not the first civilian to travel in space but he was the first to pay for the privilege. His feat was repeated the following year by South African internet millionaire Mark Shuttleworth, who paid around $20 million for a ten-day excursion on board a Russian spacecraft to the ISS.

The trips made by these millionaires are paving the way for the establishment of space hotels. British Airways and the Hilton hotel group have both shown interest in sponsoring a proposed commercial space station. The project is spear-headed by the California-based Space Island Group, who want to build a revolving space hotel. The proposed space station will be constructed from fuel tanks discharged by the space shuttles. The fuel tanks at the moment are the only part of the space shuttle that is not reused. Around twelve of the discarded containers would be joined together to form a rotating wheel. As the wheel spins it will create artificial gravity around its rim, which will make the stay more comfortable for visiting tourists. However, conditions at the center of the station would remain weightless and enable guests to experience zero gravity.

There is a tradition in the tourism industry for entrepreneurs to erect a tall tower and charge a fee to see the view from the top. Visitors to such buildings can simply enjoy the scenery or, as is the case at the Seattle Space Needle, eat in a revolving restaurant. Space tourism is likely to develop into an extreme version of this kind of attraction: the view will be magnificent but the food will probably not be as tasty. Space hotels are an exciting prospect, but they do not generate the same thrill as Gagarin's first trip into space or the Apollo lunar landing.

Over thirty years have passed since the days of Kisho Kurokawa's space-age Living Capsules, Paco Rabanne's futuristic fashions, and Verner Panton's revolutionary *Phantasy Landscape*. The futuristic style that accompanied the space age was at first inspiring, then deemed threatening, and now seems

quaint. These conflicting reactions are all found beneath the soaring arches of the Theme building at LAX. It was built in 1962 as a bold celebration of the future, but now stands as a monument to the aspirations of the past. The building was refurbished in 1997 with a new space-age theme restaurant called Encounter and a spectacular show of exterior illumination. Stepping into Encounter is like stepping into the future, but also the past. The restaurant has a wonderfully playful interior that mixes nostalgia for the first days of space travel with the futuristic styling of that era. Everything in Encounter, from the restaurant bar to the neon lighting is shaped around a blobular motif—even the muzak bubbles.

The Theme building looks out of place in daylight beside the gray uniformity of the airport car park and passenger terminal. However, the panoramic view from inside the restaurant at night is something else. All that is still becomes invisible in the darkness, while everything that can be seen is in motion. Illuminated glass towers, which circle the airport approach and line the runway, progress through a sequence of harmonious colors. Squiggles of neon streak across the restaurant ceiling and meet the navigation lights of aircraft as they disappear into the sky. The scenario is in constant flux. It could almost be the future that the Theme building once celebrated.

The Theme building and its restaurant illustrate how the style of the space age will always be around to inspire countless theme bars, restaurants, and entertainment complexes. Cynthia's Bar in London, for example, is styled around an imaginary spaceship. The interconnecting galleries that make up the bar's interior are united by the wide application of reflective materials across the walls, floor and ceiling. Beads of red and blue light pulsate around table legs and the dance floor. Cynthia herself is a robot bartender and has been programmed to mix a variety of cocktails. The overall effect is futuristic but also kitsch. In the early 1970s, the imagery that celebrated new technology

Top: Dick Becker, Cynthia's Bar and Restaurant, home of Cynthia the robotic cocktail waitress and Rastus, a second robot who presides over another bar in the complex, London Bridge, London.

BEYOND INFINITY
π
GIVENCHY

and the conquest of space was frowned upon, even feared. Cynthia's is just one example of how the futuristic imagery that once seemed so threatening is now viewed with amusement and nostalgia.

The visionaries of the 1960s often used the year 2000 as the focal point for their predictions. When the year 2000 did arrive, it provided a pivotal moment in time to look back at those ideas and take stock of what we have—or have not—achieved since. The decade preceding the year 2000 was a festival of nostalgia and designers from all disciplines plundered the recent past in search of inspiration. This resulted in the rediscovery of the space-age style that had been abandoned since the early 1970s.

Architects and designers who were last prominent in the 1960s have suddenly become fashionable again. There is a resurgence of interest in the work of Verner Panton, Archigram, Eero Aarnio and their contemporaries. The futuristic outfits of Paco Rabanne, Pierre Cardin, and André Courrèges are a major influence on the work of new designers including Sophia Kokosalaki and Roland Mouret. Givenchy, too, has used a heroic astronaut figure in the poster campaign for its *Pi* fragrance.

Plastic, the material that shaped the space age, has also undergone a revival of interest. Eero Aarnio produced his new *Formula* chair in 1998. This was a synthetic celebration of speed and marked a return for the designer to the flowing lines he employed in the *Pastil* and *Tomato* chair thirty years earlier. A glossy red *Panton* chair appeared on the cover of *Vogue* magazine in 1995 with a naked Kate Moss draped over it. Vitra resumed manufacture and retail of the legendary chair in 1990 and Verner Panton developed a new version made of injection-molded polypropylene, which was launched in 1999. Panton died in September 1998, twelve days before the opening of the first major exhibition of his work at the Trapholtmuseum, Denmark, titled *Verner Panton: Light and Color*, which Panton himself designed.

In 1998, film director Mika Taanila told the story of Matti Suuronen's plastic house in the acclaimed documentary *Futuro: A New Stance for Tomorrow*. The film raised many questions about the utopian future that was promised at the height of the space age and how quickly such promises were forgotten. The documentary closes on the poignant image of one of the few remaining Futuro houses, which stands neglected in a children's playground in Estonia. Taanila's film expresses sadness for Futuro and the future it was supposed to deliver, but also a tremendous sense of loss for the optimistic spirit that created it. It was the childlike belief in the future that, after years of doubt and skepticism, now seems so refreshing.

The renewed interest in the futuristic style of the 1960s resulted in a new generation of designers and

Opposite: Poster campaign for Givenchy's Pi fragrance, 2002.

Top: Philippe Starck, *Strange Thing* armchair, manufactured by Cassina, Italy, 2002.

Center: Eero Aarnio, *Formula* chair, 1998.

Right: Aleksej Iskos, *Ground Floor* chair, 2000.

architects drawing inspiration from that distinct period. Following the example set by Verner Panton and Eero Aarnio are the *Ground Floor* chair (2000) by Aleksej Iskos and the *Vector* chaise longue (2002) by Fly Pitcher. Both pieces are fabricated from a single material and can be stacked to save space. The undulating curves that form the seat of *Ground Floor* rise from a flat sheet of plastic and celebrate the synthetic material's versatility. *Vector* is sharp and angular, it looks violent in comparison yet both chairs exude the slickness and dynamism of their space-age ancestors.

The chairs *Strange Thing* (2002), designed by Philippe Stark for Italian firm, Cassina, and *Global Cruiser* (2002), designed by Alexander Lotersztain for Tokyo-based collective, Sputnik, follow the example of softer, foam-filled pieces of space-age furniture. The spongy *Global Cruiser* looks like it might take off at any moment and the tapered legs of *Strange Thing* could almost run away. Both use foam to create

Top: Philippe Starck, *Strange Thing* sofa, manufactured by Cassina, Italy, 2002.

Bottom right: Fly Pitcher, *Vector* chaise longue, 2002, and *Estate* lamp, 2002. Integral skin urethane foam; optional chrome-plated steel swivel base.

Bottom left: Alexander Lotersztain, *Global Cruiser* armchair, manufactured by Sputnik/IDEE Co Ltd., Tokyo, Japan, 2002.

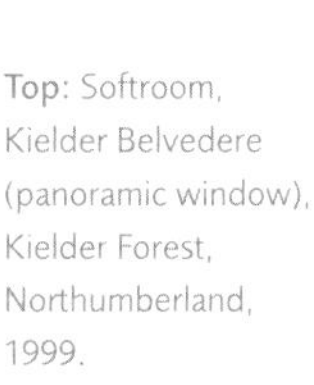

Top: Softroom, Kielder Belvedere (panoramic window), Kielder Forest, Northumberland, 1999.

Right: Softroom, Kielder Belvedere (cross section), Kielder Forest, Northumberland, 1999.

informal seating elements and are reminiscent of the chairs by Pierre Paulin and Olivier Mourgue.

Away from furniture design, the futuristic style is also finding its way into architecture and some unlikely locations. The English countryside might be regarded as a bastion of tradition, but even here, a number of startling architectural projects have recently taken shape. Tokyo-based architects Ushida Findlay won a competition in January 2002 to design and build Grafton Hall, a new generation of English country house. Ushida Findlay's work is characterized by free-flowing curves and rounded spaces. The practice is well known for its radical sculpted dwellings, such as the Truss Wall House (1991–93) in Machida-City, Japan. Like the futuristic designers of the 1960s, Ushida Findlay marry organic forms with high-tech production methods to create unusual buildings that look as if they have

been grown rather than built. The wings of Grafton Hall spread out to form a large star shape and create a home that is not like any building seen before in the tradition-loving English countryside.

A smaller-scale, but no less impressive building, is Kielder Belvedere (1999), by London-based architects Softroom. The shelter looks like a space-age sentry post and sits on an exposed slope overlooking Kielder Water, a large man-made lake in Northumberland, England. This shining example of ultra-modern styling acts as a rest-stop for walkers enjoying the countryside. The plan of the shelter is a truncated triangle, with a doorway forming the blunt end. The two walls facing the woodland path are made up of etched steel mirrors and reflect the forest scenery. The third wall overlooks the lake and is formed by a dramatic concave mirror, which reflects the water and sky.

The triangular exterior masks a circular, drum-like interior, in the center of which sits a bench facing a curved, strip window offering panoramic views over the lake. A tinted skylight and the yellow walls warm the interior with a golden glow. From the outside, the curved panoramic window looks like a flat cord that has been threaded through the reflective wall and given a sudden yank, causing it to cave in slightly. If it were pulled any tighter it would rip the wall clean from its foundations. The triangular plan and the illusory tension of the concave wall gives the shelter a tremendous sense of energy. Far from looking out of place in the natural environment the futuristic shelter blends seamlessly with it. The lake and its surroundings may appear natural but the area is a man-made nature park. Kielder Belvedere celebrates the coming together of nature and

Top: Softroom, Kielder Belvedere (entrance), Kielder Forest, Northumberland, 1999. The stucture operates as a shelter for walkers and passengers waiting to board the ferry to cross the lake.

technology, and its striking form makes no attempt to hide among the trees.

One of the most fascinating aspects of the space-age revival has been the resurrection of the living pod. The new wave of condensed environments are made with a variety of materials ranging from inflatable PVC to disused cement mixers. The new pods also serve a variety of functions, some provide a place of refuge, whereas others are high-tech leisure lounges. A capsule is interesting because of its ability to provide an intimate space where the old rules no longer apply. It can be used as a sanctuary of calm away from everyday commotion, or offer an intense experience with the real world acting as a safety net to return to.

Chill Out Room by Australian firm Room Interiors and *Cloud* by Scandinavian studio Snowcrash are both inflatable capsules offering a refuge from reality. The exterior of *Chill Out Room* resembles a spherical honeycomb and is made up of thirty-one inflatable hexagonal pillows. Inside, following in the tradition of Haus-Rucker-Co's *Gelbes Herz*, there is an intimate space for two people to escape from the outside world and relax. *Cloud*, designed by Monica Förster for Snowcrash, is made of rip-stop nylon and possesses a rare ethereal quality. Unlike *Chill Out Room*, which is

Above: Room Interiors, *Chill Out Room*, Australia, 2000.

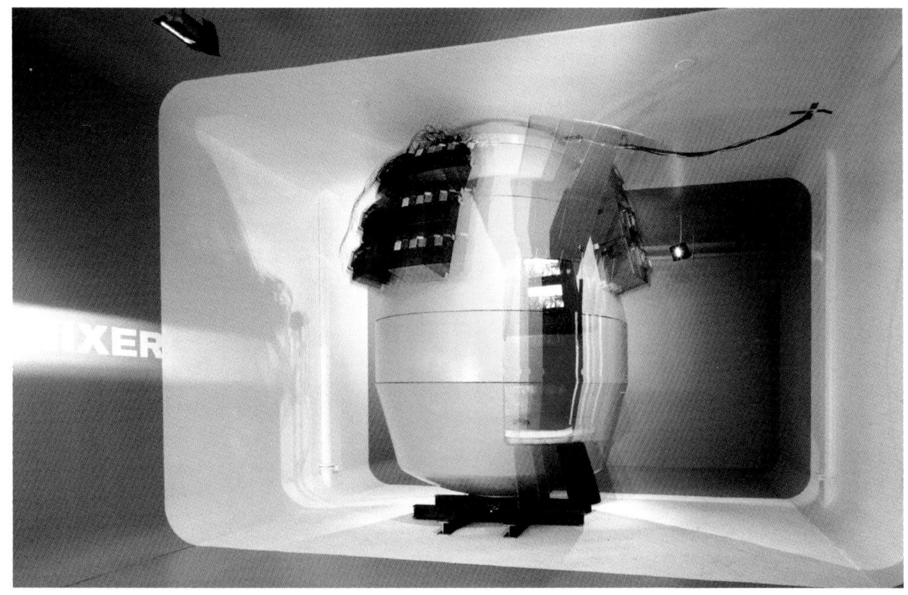

supported by a network of separately inflated cushions, *Cloud* is a single skin structure supported by the air inside it and has its own fan to keep it blown up. Snowcrash describe *Cloud* as "a portable room for rest, meeting or concentration. A space of its own that can be used within any space, *Cloud* instantly defines an area and a mood apart." In the fashionable open-plan loft apartments and homes of the early 21st century, these rather exclusive inflatable chambers provide an enclosed personal space.

Mixer (2000), created by New York-based architects LOT/EK, is a completely different proposition to *Cloud* and *Chill Out Room*. The capsule is made from an upturned yellow drum taken from the back of a large cement-mixing truck. The discarded industrial container is transformed into a condensed entertainment complex with enough space to accommodate four people. The padded interior is a futuristic leisure-lounge complete with television, music system, and games console. The cement-mixing drum is a ready-made container and its walls separate the people inside from the world outside. There are no windows, but a series of CCTV cameras positioned around the capsule's exterior feed images to the monitors inside. *Mixer* is physically sealed from the outside world yet remains connected to it through an electronic link formed by the cameras, television, and also an internet station. The pod is a total experience environment and enables its user to escape to another world.

LOT/EK's *TV Tank* (1999) is a similar device and sees an oil tank transformed into a TV lounge. The end result resembles a video game arcade. Incisions were made in the former oil container to leave a row of comfortable pods, each with its own monitor. *TV Tank* and *Mixer* are the result of an inventive fusion between old and new technology. LOT/EK are passionate about finding new and unexpected

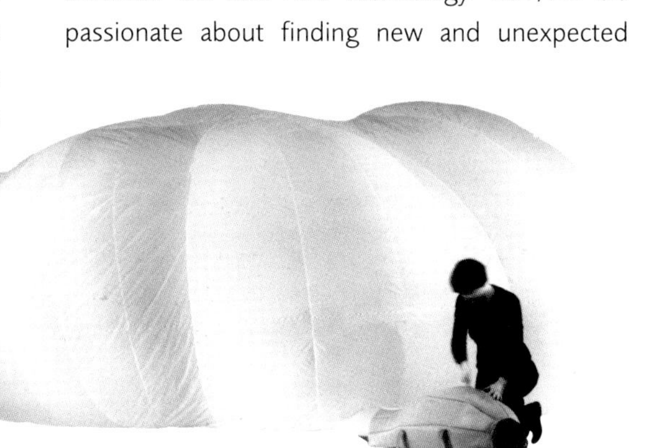

Top: LOT/EK, *Mixer*. A steel cement mixer transformed into a 21st-century media cocoon fitted with advanced technological equipment. The 3.6 x 2.1-meter, 1,361-kilo yellow pod made from a cement mixer to house two people, contains DVD player, 12 monitors, surround sound, and Playstation 2. For $70,000 you can have one custom built in your home.

Left: Monica Förster, *Cloud*, manufactured by Snowcrash, Sweden, 2002.

Right and opposite: LOT/EK, TV Tank. A petroleum trailer tank transformed into a set of floating modules designed for lounging and watching television. The 10.6-meter aluminum tank was sliced into eight rings, each module then retrofitted with a liner of rubber tubing and a 33-centimeter color television equipped with cable and remote control. Viewers recline inside the once-hidden interior of the oil tank, now animated by the flicker of television light.

applications for industrial relics. The studio was established in 1992 by Ada Tolla and Giuseppe Lignano and has since revitalized all kinds of industrial relics by inserting them into the domestic environment. "Our vision," stated Tolla in an interview with Christopher Hawthorne of *Metropolis* magazine, "and you could even call it our obsession, is to explore what happens when you combine an older object with cutting edge technology." *TV Tank* and *Mixer* are typical of LOT/EK's work in that discarded industrial objects have been transformed with a new purpose, while the container's history remains on full show.

Spanish artist Martín Ruiz de Azua takes a critical approach to modern living and uses his capsule, *Basic House* (1998), to question the amount of material possessions we fill our homes with. The simple inflatable shelter strips the fabric of the home to its most basic elements. The capsule is made with a double-sided, metallic fabric, which bears close resemblance to the material used to protect satellites in the extreme environment of space. *Basic House* recalls Archigram's *Suitaloon* and once inflated, it seems weightless.

A capsule with more sinister connotations is the *Faraday Chair* (1995–98) by Anthony Dunne and Fiona Raby. The unit comes from a series of prototype devices that draw attention to "Hertzian space", the electromagnetic environ-ment formed by radar waves, electronic goods and radio trans-missions. It is a relatively recent addition to our environment and has expanded enormously since the advent of satellite communications. The *Faraday Chair* is coated with a conductive film that shields the inhabitant from electromagnetic waves. The restricted confines of the capsule are cramped and awkward and highlight the value of the unpolluted area inside. The chair is physically uncomfortable yet mentally restful because, once inside, one no longer need worry about bombardment from electromagnetic radiation.

In another proposal entitled *Pillow* (1995–98), Dunne and Raby have created a device that increases awareness of Hertzian space. Inside the inflatable cushion is an LCD screen encased in a fluorescent plastic block, from which an aerial emerges. The aerial picks up fluctuations in local radio frequencies, such as those transmitted by cordless telephones, and transforms the signals into a visual pattern on the LCD screen. Additionally, the device emits distorted sounds from the signals and, if one presses one's ear against the pillow, the actual transmitted conver-sations can be heard. *Pillow* questions the notion of privacy in the electro-magnetic environment. It is often illegal to listen in on someone else's telephone call, but there are few restrictions on the radiation from that call invading another person's home and body. *Faraday Chair* and *Pillow* expresses a need for us all to gain a greater understanding of the electromagnetic realm that surrounds us.

This page and opposite: Martín Ruiz de Azua, *Basic House*, 1998. Made from a metallic material similar to that used to coat satellites, *Basic House* reduces the structure of the house to the fundamental elements of floor, walls, and ceiling. Air is the main structural element and this gives the house an appearance of weightlessness. It can be erected anywhere and reduces down to fit inside a pocket.

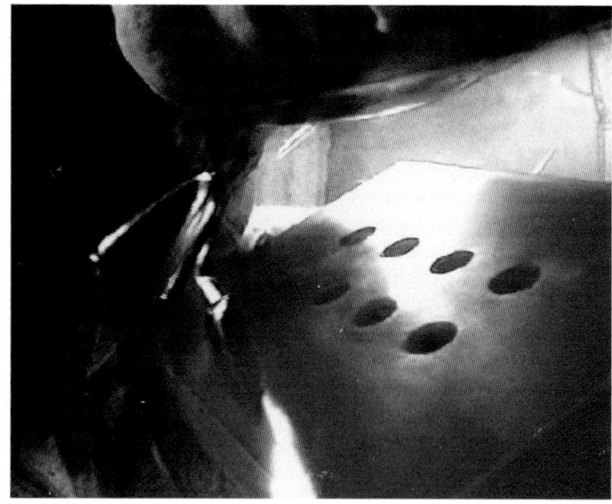

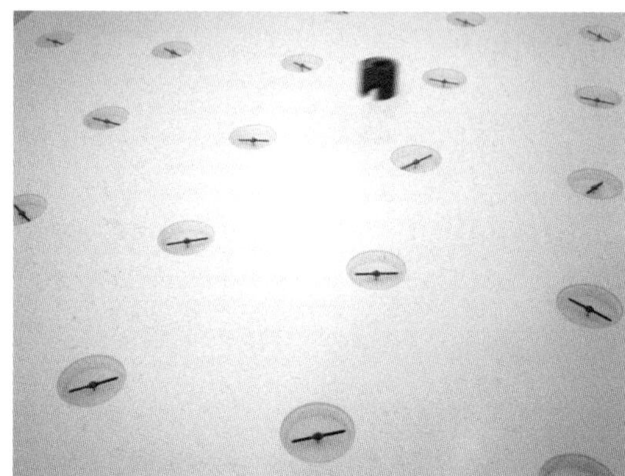

Similar concerns about the need to proceed into the future with caution are expressed in the work of Kenji Yanobe. The contemporary Japanese artist creates futuristic capsules, vehicles, and suits, but these are not for busy commuters in an ultra-modern metropolis, they are survival systems for use in the aftermath of a nuclear catastrophe. Yanobe's work is the flip side to the technological utopia represented by Expo '70 in Osaka. He once described himself as the "last son of the bubble

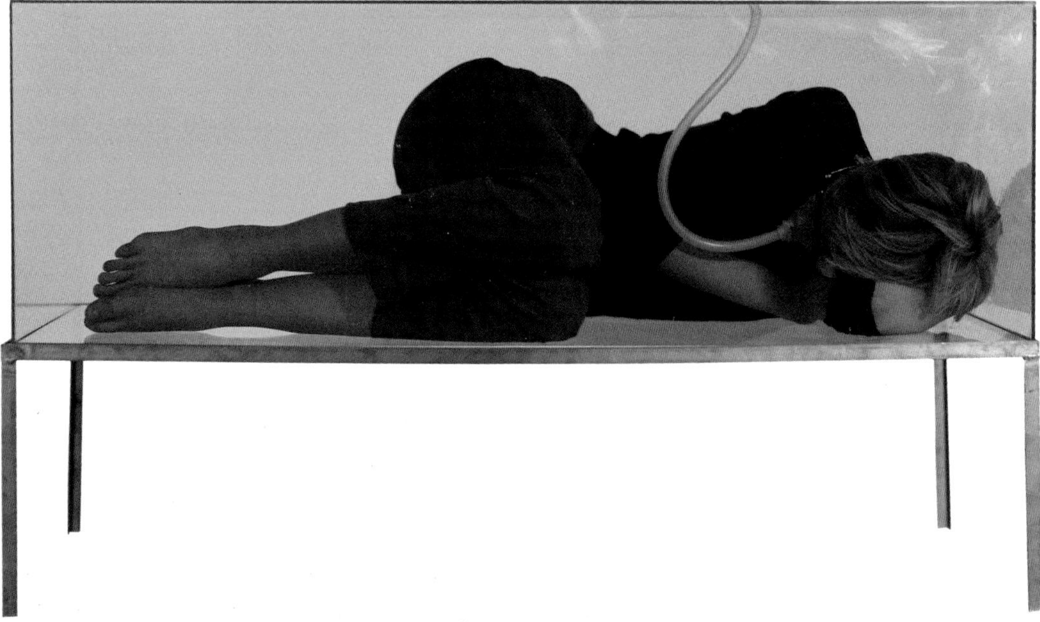

Top: Dunne and Raby, *Pillow*, 1995–98.

Center: Dunne and Raby, *Compass Table*, 1995–98.

Bottom: Dunne and Raby, *Faraday Chair*, 1995–98.

period in Japan" and his work is a clear reminder of how the euphoric visions of the space age have descended into fear and paranoia.

The Osaka festival site was very close to Yanobe's family home. As a young child he witnessed the sensational event and also its demise. The demolished remains of Expo '70 are a major influence on Yanobe's work. He recalls: "I used to play in the ruins of the Expo, with its destroyed robots, strange scientific pavilions, and spacey sculptures. The huge hall was deserted. I became interested in the image of ruins after a big futuristic catastrophe." Pieces such as *Atom Car, White* (1998) and *Emergency Escape Pod* (1996) recall the futuristic visions presented at the Expo and would not look out of place if they were exhibited there. However, despite Yanobe's obvious fascination for futuristic gadgetry, his work conveys a deep-rooted fear of high-technology and its implications for the future. The artist's paranoid vision would not sit at all well alongside the playful speculation of Kurokawa's Takara Beautilion or the Sanyo *Living Capsule*. *Atom Car, White* (1998) is strangely reminiscent of Sanyo's *Ultrasonic Bath*, one of the company's most popular exhibits at Expo '70. The egg-like casing of the human washing machine could almost have been dismantled and reassembled to form *Atom Car, White*'s bubble-shaped bodywork and driver's cab. The function of the two devices is also very similar as both are concerned with decontamination—*Ultrasonic Bath* washes away dirt and *Atom Car, White* keeps its driver free from radioactive dust. The vehicle, like many other examples of Yanobe's work, is equipped with a Geiger counter to monitor levels of radiation. It is a reminder that Japan's economic bubble expanded from the radioactive ruins of Hiroshima and Nagasaki. Yanobe also cites the 1991 accident at Mihama Nuclear Power Plant, Fukui, as another major influence on his art. It occurred at a time when the artist was thinking about the relevance of his work to his own situation and that of his family. As a consequence of the accident and other nuclear tragedies, Yanobe began inventing devices that might protect his family from the physical damage caused by radioactive fallout.

The living capsules presented at Expo '70 in the Takara Beautilion and the Sanyo pavilion were small units with all the comforts of home. They provided a refuge—complete with entertainment system and mini-bar—for the individual in a busy urban metropolis. The capsules looked forward to a high-tech future of movement and change. Yanobe's *Tanking Machine* (1997) and *Emergency Escape Pod* (1997) take that utopian ideal and inject it with some late 20th-century paranoia. These capsules are not intended to facilitate a busy modern lifestyle —they are tools for extreme survival. The pods are

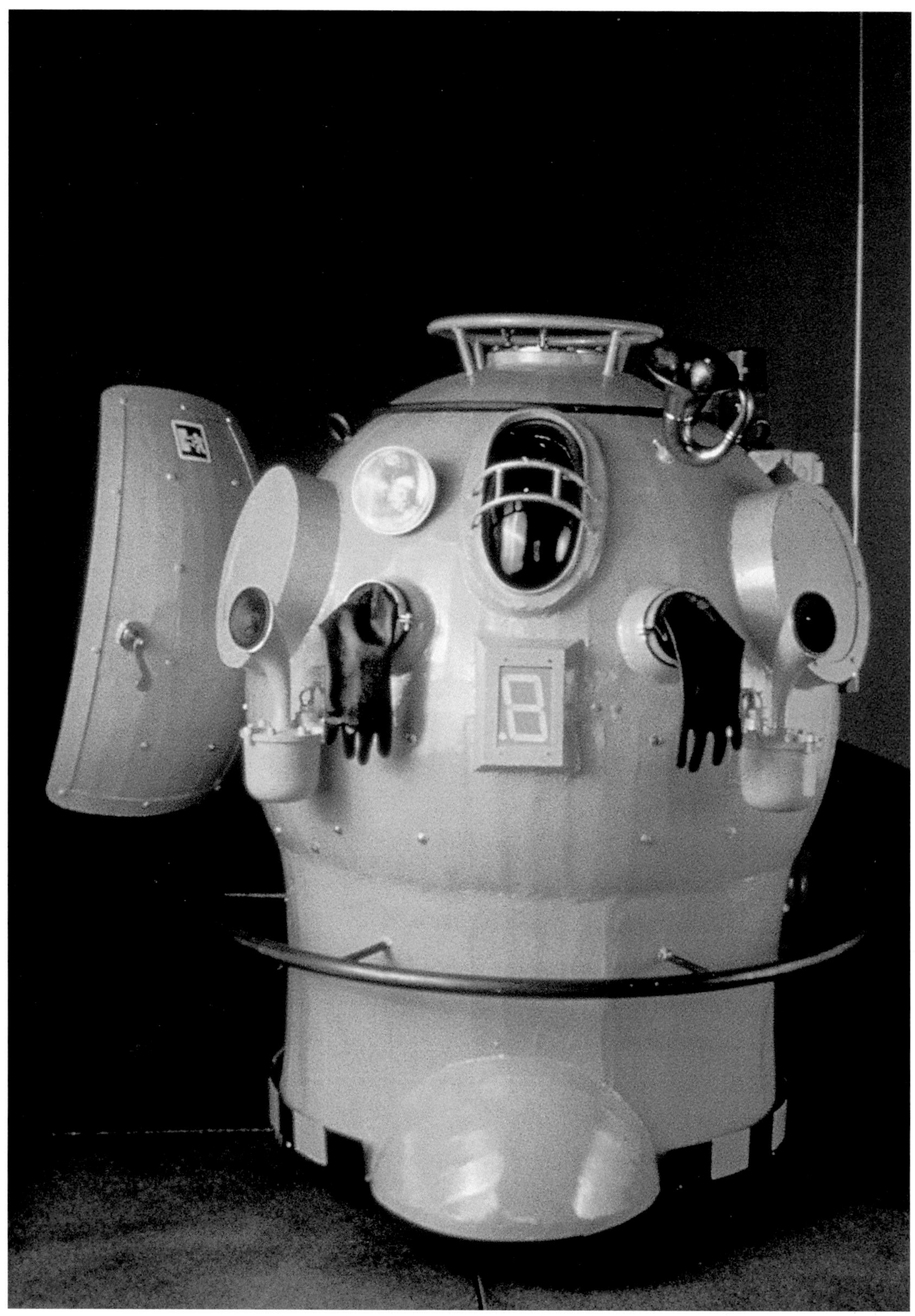

Right:
Kenji Yanobe,
Emergency Escape Pod, 1997.

equipped with the essentials of food and water and provide a safe haven from the apocalyptic aftermath of a nuclear explosion. As a child, Yanobe witnessed the destruction of the Expo '70 site, which represented a vision of tomorrow that never arrived and was left surrounded by defunct robots and other futuristic contraptions.

Radiation Suit, Atom (1996) and *Radiation Suit, Uran* (1996) are his-and-her suits of radiation-shielding body armor. The outfits resemble primitive EVA suits and are similarly designed to cope with an extreme environment. The outfits include radiation-monitoring devices to measure exposure around the vital organs—precautions that should ensure any children conceived among atomic ruins of the future are not born suffering with radiation sickness.

Despite all the sinister connotations of Yanobe's work, there is also a comic element to it. His contraptions rattle around producing cartoon-like gestures and exaggerated sounds. He is a big fan of science fiction, especially *manga* (Japanese comic books and animation) and this is a major influence on his work. His childhood experiences were informed by Godzilla and Japanese cartoon shows, and these influences are as real to Yanobe as any historical event or work of art.

In the philosophy of Metabolism, Kurokawa sought methods of harnessing new technology and bringing it into harmony with human existence.

Left:
Kenji Yanobe at the Gösgen nuclear power station, Switzerland, April 1997.

Kenji Yanobe, on the other hand, creates devices that offer protection in the nightmarish scenario of technology gone haywire. His vehicles, capsules, and body suits act as a refuge from the devastation of a nuclear accident or attack. His work is rooted in a simple faith in technology and a desire for progress, but reveals a growing apprehension in the face of what it might deliver.

Where Yanobe's art fears the misuse of high-technology, the work of one of his contemporaries, Mariko Mori, suggests that when harnessed appropriately, it will deliver great things. Mori samples and remixes images from the past, present, and future in works of art that reference Buddhist philosophy, Western art history, popular culture and Japanese tradition. The Expo '70 theme of "Progress and Harmony for Mankind" aptly describes the chief concern of her work. Mori calls for a future of progress and harmony not through the consumption of electronic appliances, but the union of art, technology, and spirituality. She once stated in an interview with Margery King that "technology always changes history dramatically. It has opened up and changed not only our lifestyle, but probably our way of thinking, and even our philosophy and consciousness."

In early examples of Mori's work, such as the photographs *Subway* (1994) and *Play With Me* (1994), the artist depicts herself wearing futuristic costumes amid routine scenes of Tokyo life. In *Subway* Mori presents herself in a metallic body suit on a subway train. The shot is taken through a very wide-angled lens and we can see the other passengers in the carriage. Although Mori looks as though she has just arrived from another planet, nobody pays her much attention. The carriage doors are open and behind her on the platform a small group of commuters seem amused by her bizarre outfit. The image is alive with motion. The doors are about to slam shut. The train is about to depart. Mori looks up and her long black hair sweeps across her silver shoulders. She is about to punch in a command on the keypad fastened to her sleeve. Her costume resembles utility wear and she looks like a space trooper ready for action. This is a sharp contrast to the submissive character Mori plays in *Play With Me*. Here she poses as a futuristic fantasy girl waiting to be picked up outside a *manga* arcade. Her hair is arranged in cute bunches and she wears a suit of space-age body armor, but again, she is not paid any attention by the comic-shop customers.

Manga is big business in Japan with many thousands of avid fans and collectors. The really hardcore fans are known as *otaku*. Their obsession with fantasy worlds depicted in *manga* provides escapism from reality. Mori has turned that idea around and injected a fantasy character into a real life situation. In *Play With Me*, the artist represents the kind of girl the *manga* fans in the store might fantasize over. Their dream girl has arrived from a

Right: Thomas Stricker, *Mission—Terraforming als Happy End*, 2001. Styropor foam, plaster, video surveillance camera, joystick, monitor, overhead projection, diameter of ball, 2.34 m. Viewers are able to explore the sculpture's interior with a remote-control video camera linked to a projector. Stricker created the sphere originally as the cast for a sculpture of a meteorite in the public project *Aussendienst*, Hamburger Kunstverein, 2000. The spherical cast, in addition to the temporary studio where Stricker was working at the time, was conceived as a sculpture in its own right. Its interior is the reverse form of the meteorite sculpture and, when viewed via the camera, the illuminated craters on its surface resemble the surface of another planet.

fictional future and is waiting outside, but they all walk past and ignore her. She wants to play but nobody wants to play with her. Fiction and reality have merged outside a comic shop

Unlike Yanobe, Mori employs the very latest imaging technology in the creation of her art. As advances in this area have progressed so too has Mori's work. *Subway* and *Play With Me* have the look of a real situation and in them Mori's characters are flesh and blood. In later works, such as *Last Departure* and *Miko No Inori (Link of the Moon)* (both 1996) her image is digitally enhanced and she makes a convincing transformation from earthling to celestial being. *Last Departure*, like *Subway* and *Play With Me*, is set in a real place—the Kansai International Airport, Osaka. However, in Mori's photograph the passenger terminal is treated in such a way that it becomes an unreal location. Like *Subway*, the location Mori has placed herself in is the scene of arrivals and departures. No one settles at airport terminal, it is a place of transition.

Mori depicts herself with two ghost images

Top:
Mariko Mori, *Play With Me*, 1994.
Fuji super gloss (duraflex) print, wood, pewter frame 305 x 366 x 7.5cm.

standing by her side. She wears a reflective, space-age outfit consisting of white, knee-high boots, metallic blue tights, and a white miniskirt and top. The costume is completed by a set of inflated, wing-like forms, comprising of two small, tapered shapes at her waist and two large ones ballooning from her chest like overblown lapels. The steely-blue colouring of the airport's interior is reflected in Mori's outfit and the long, white, ceiling canopies are echoed in the shape and colour of the inflated lapels. Suspended between the palms of her hands is a crystal ball, in which the whole scene is replicated and made infinite. Her eyes are dark blue and her blank expression suggests she is communicating with another dimension.

Last Departure accompanies the mesmerizing video installation *Miko no Inori* which was shot at the same location and shows the artist dressed in the same outfit. In the video, an enchanting song is heard over footage of Mori manipulating the transparent sphere between her hands. She seems to be in a transcendental state, like a shaman communicating with the other side. The title of both works and the futuristic styling suggest not only

space travel, but also journeys into a higher state of consciousness. Through meditation we can travel anywhere we like. The spirit leaves the body and transcends into other dimensions.

Mori expresses great faith in the future, a sentiment that is underlined by a statement she made in the catalogue for the 1997 Venice Biennale: "All living beings are connected at every moment in inner space. Every life form with its own life cycle is part of the outer universe and there is only one planet Earth. In the next millennium, the power and energy of the human spirit should unify the world in peace and harmony without any cultural or national borders." Mori uses an accessible visual language to communicate these ideals and in so doing offers an utopian image of the future, in a fusion of ideas and icons from both the present and the past.

Both Mori and Yanobe play with the boundaries between fiction and reality, questioning where history

ends and fantasy begins. They are rep-resentatives of a generation that has grown up in the synthesized environment of television and computer games. Such artists are able to sample historic events as easily as contemporary fashions and popular culture, without differentiating between the two. The Apollo moon landing was a defining moment in the childhoods of many artists who are now reaching maturity. Recent

Top: Mariko Mori, *Subway*, 1994, Fuji supergloss (duraflex) print 68.6 x 102cm.

Above: Mariko Mori, *Miko no Inori (Link of the Moon)*, video still, 1996.

Right: Aleksandra Mir, *First Woman on the Moon*, performance, land art, media spectacle, produced by Casco Projects, Utrecht, on location in Wijk aan Zee, Netherlands, August 28, 1999.

Top:
Andrew Grassie,
Untitled (Why Paint Spacemen), 1997.
Oil on canvas on board, each 28.5 x 21 cm.

years have seen a number of such artists draw directly on events and images that surrounded them in the first years of the space age. On August 28, 1999, a beach at Wijk aan Zee in the Netherlands, was transformed by mechanical diggers into a crater-filled lunar landscape. It was in this moonscape by the sea that artist Aleksandra Mir staged the happening *First Woman on the Moon*. Local people, camera crews, photographers, art fans, and holiday-makers, watched on as the flat beach by the North Sea was sculpted into an earthbound Sea of Tranquillity. In the evening, the appropriately named Mir and a group of "astronettes" enacted their own lunar landing while children played among the giant sand castles. The event culminated with the artist climbing a crater wall in her own spacesuit and planting the American flag. The bulldozers moved in a few moments later and the beach was restored as if nothing had happened.

Mir examines issues that were prevalent in the 1960s, such as women's liberation, the civil rights movement, and anti-war demonstrations, and explores how they sit together today. Her own staging of the lunar landing raises questions of gender and public spectacle. *First Woman on the Moon*, like the first Apollo moon landing, was recorded and transmitted in still and moving pictures. Mir's performance was a low-budget recreation and questioned the role of the media in the shaping of historic events. The television images, photographs, and sound recordings of the Apollo mission have engraved it vividly on the memories of millions. It was the first global media event. Nobody was up there to watch it "live" so television was used to bring a new version of reality into the home. The Apollo moon landing and Mir's own interpretation were stage-managed performances of real events. Technology and entertainment were combined to stage a public spectacle. Conspiracy theorists suggest the Apollo images are lies and that no man has ever set foot on the moon. Perhaps one of the reasons why the conspiracy theorists have their doubts is precisely because of the way the event was managed for a television audience.

Paul Ramírez Jonas is another artist to have drawn on the Apollo 11 mission to the moon. He presented an installation entitled *Man on the Moon Parts IV and V* (1990) at the Whitechapel Art Gallery in London. For the installation, Jonas remastered recordings of the communications between the Apollo 11 spacecraft and Houston ground control onto old-fashioned wax cylinders, the kind used in gramophone machines. Hundreds of these cylinders, each holding approximately one minute of recorded sound, were stacked on shelves across a wall in the gallery. The act consigns the lunar landing even further back into history and suggests that the technology that took men to the moon is now primitive and dated.

Left:
Andrew Grassie,
Untitled (Why Paint Spacemen), 1997.
Oil on canvas on board, 28.5 x 21cm.

Top:
Bryan Cyril Griffiths, *Laika Belka*, 1997. Installation at MC Magma, Milan, Italy, February 26–April 13, 2002. Cardboard, wood, and household junk.

London-based painter Andrew Grassie also used excerpts of dialogue from the Apollo 11 mission and displayed the quotations alongside a series of paintings entitled *Landscapes Without UFOs*. The source material for the paintings, which include *Fir Tree Hinterland* (1999) and *Alpine Scene* (1999), came from photographs of the landscapes found by the artist on the internet. The painted scenes may appear ordinary, but are all locations of alleged UFO sightings. Grassie also used the internet as the source material for a series of astronaut portraits he painted in 1997 under the collective title, *Why Paint Spacemen?* The portraits, which include *Alan Bean* (1997) and *Charles "Pete" Conrad* (1997) have the look of enlarged bubble-gum cards, the kind of ephemera that surrounded the space race. The astronauts look like ordinary guys, but they were made extraordinary by their achievements in space. Grassie is completely faithful to the online pictures and includes all the peculiarities in his paintings that characterize a digital

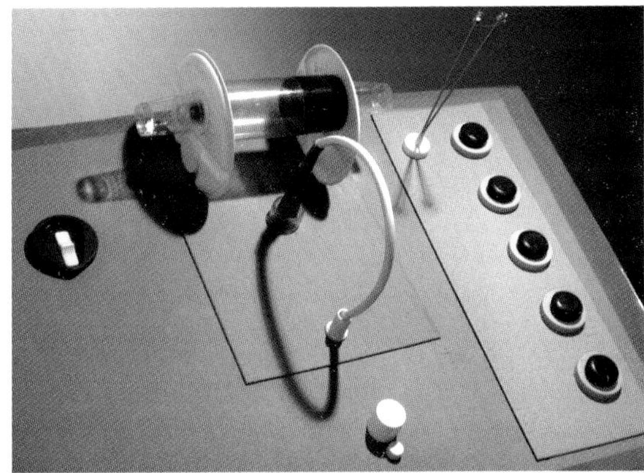

Top left:
Brian Cyril Griffiths, *Laika Belka* (detail), 1997. Installation at MC Magma, Milan, Italy, February 26–April 13, 2002.

Top right:
Brian Cyril Griffiths, *Once upon a Star*, 1999. Expanding polystyrene foam.

image, such as pixelation and flat planes of color.

The image of an astronaut floating free in space is one of the most vivid sights of the late 20th century. The reflective solar visor renders the astronaut faceless and anybody looking at such an image can easily impose their own identity on to it. Even though the astronaut is alone in the extreme environment of space he seems safe, like an unborn child curled up in the womb, the final powerful image of Stanley Kubrick's 1968 film, *2001: A Space Odyssey*. The image of the individual astronaut is applied to many different situations and encompasses a wide range of interpretations. For some it represents freedom and mankind's greatest achievement, for others it was a mere public relations exercise and a big waste of money.

At the turn of the new millennium, two London-based artists, Fergal Stapleton and Brian Cyril Griffiths sculpted two very different interpretations of an astronaut. One a small, clay model, the other a

Right:
Yinka Shonibare
Vacation, 2000.
Wax printed cotton textile, fiberglass figures, plastic.
2 figures c. 152.5 x 61 x 61 cm; 2 figures c. 106.6 x 61 x 61 cm.
Shonibare (1962–) takes an astronaut family, dressed in African-style cloth, to question the traditional idea of the single white male astronaut, overlaid with thoughts about families, space tourism, and cultural imperialism.

fat, expanded-foam and polystyrene effigy. The two sculptures depict one of the most enduring icons of recent history and display a variety of reactions to it. They were created over the transition from one millennium to the next, a period of contemplation of the past and the future. Stapleton's *Fergal* (2000) seems fragile and childlike, as if it had been the artist's boyhood dream to be an astronaut. Griffiths's *Once Upon a Star* (1999) is made with synthetic foam, the revolutionary plastic that helped shape the space age and establish the throwaway society. Its form is swollen and grotesque, like the orgy of consumption that landed a man on the moon.

In other examples of his work, Brian Cyril Griffiths has used an array of disposable products to build space age environments. In the installation *Laika Belka* (1997), Griffiths converted a room in the City Racing gallery, London, into the control deck of a space station. He made all the instruments and panels out of everyday junk, such as cardboard

boxes, paper plates, pencils and kitchen utensils. A similar piece was also installed at MC Magma, Milan, Italy in February 2002. In these works Griffiths finds ulterior uses for everyday things. *Laika Belka* is like a grown-up version of the scenario a child might construct in his bedroom, but it is characterized by meticulous attention to detail.

The installation seems nostalgic for the early years of space travel as well as low-budget, science fiction TV series with shaky sets and improvised props. There seems to be an enormous sense of loss in these installations. A great deal of effort has obviously gone into their construction, but they speak of the fragility of the playground: in an instant the school bully could destroy it with a kick, or a parent might throw it away by mistake. In the end the control panels will never function as a space station no matter how hard Griffith concentrates his efforts.

Artists who were children at the time of the space race seem intent on converting feats of high-

Above:
Fergal Stapleton,
Fergal, 2000.
Clay and paint.

Right:
Yinka Shonibare, *Alien Obsessives, Mum, Dad and the Kids*, 1998.
Wax printed cotton, plastic and polyester fiberfill on plastic and metal armatures. Eight figures. Installation dimensions variable. Shonibare, whose work appeared in the 1997 Sensation exhibition at London's Royal Academy, has in this piece turned the nuclear family—decked out in African-style cloth—into aliens. Here space-age imagery contributes to an exploration of otherness and cultural identity.

technology into older formats from childhood that they can understand. Andrew Grassie paints digital images that he could just as easily print out, Aleksandra Mir uses diggers and sand to create a moonscape she could have molded in virtual reality, and Brian Cyril Griffiths builds space stations out of cardboard when its real assembly would require an array of computers. The art works mentioned here draw inspiration from the early years of space travel, when it was still a public spectacle. It is as if they are trying to make sense of those events by breaking them down into a simplified form. There is still as much confusion about the trip to the moon as there ever has been. The lunar landing was a defining moment in history, but people are still unsure of their feelings toward it. These feelings are further complicated by the fact that outer space was a battlefield of the Cold War.

The American journeys into space are well documented, but the Soviet space program remains a comparative mystery. Russian victories in space are well documented, but not backed up with potent images. In sharp contrast, the activities of NASA were heavily photographed—even down to the private lives of the astronauts. Few photographs exist of Yuri Gagarin's lift-off into space or his return to earth. His words from space were recorded but there are no photographs to illustrate those words. The stage management of the Soviet campaign was not as effective as NASA's, but it still made an impact. The Soviet space program was always shrouded in secrecy, which now fills it with intrigue.

Since the end of the Cold War, there has been an influx of artists eager to find out what went on behind the Iron Curtain. It always seemed so gray and colorless, an oppressive environment ruled by factory-made uniformity. The photographer Adam Bartos produced a magnificent retrospective of the Soviet space program, published in his book *Kosmos: A Portrait of the Russian Space Age*. He visited launch sites, assembly plants, and training

Above:
Adam Bartos, *Oleg Ivanovsky's Memorabilia*, Moscow, 1996. The photograph on the right shows Ivanovsky helping cosmonaut Yuri Gagarin into his space capsule before closing the hatch.

Left: Adam Bartos, *Selection of Yuri Frumkin's Badge Collection*, Moscow, 1997. Yuri Frumkin specialized in the design of reconnaissance satellites.

Right:
Børre Sæthre, *My Private Sky—Lobby*, 2001.
Sæthre is known for his total experience environments that provide an unsettling experience in a contained space away from the real world. The Lobby area has the feel of a passenger terminal and acts as a point of departure into the sealed *Explosion Suite*, a series of corridors that is revealed by the automated opening of a sliding door. The installation resembles a space station, but its slick, clinical finish is a far cry from the cardboard console of Griffiths' *Laika Belka*.

centers, photographed souvenirs and medals, and former cosmonauts who helped score so many victories for their leaders. The collection of photographs highlights the contradictions of the Soviet space program, which defined the USSR's identity and transformed the international perception of the super power. Even in the early 1990s such a project would have been unthinkable, but the end of the Cold War revealed some of the stories that had been hidden for so long.

The Cold War has also provided a rich vein of source material for the installation artists Jane and Louise Wilson. The sisters were invited by the DAAD to spend a year in the once divided city of Berlin in 1996. The German capital was the front line of the Cold War, the scene of espionage, political intrigue, conspiracy, torture, and murder. It was here that the artists embarked on the project *Stasi City* (1997), a film shot in the former offices of the Stasi, the East German secret police, and in Höhenschonhausen, a former Stasi prison. The Stasi complex was used as a prison and interrogation center for political prisoners. The film draws on its claustrophobic atmosphere in a reference to what the artists describe as the "confinement of East Berlin."

A uniformed figure floats through certain scenes of the film as if the building is free from the forces of gravity. The scenario draws a parallel between the notion that citizens of communist East Berlin were expected to cheer as their comrades circled the Earth, yet they could not even cross the street into the West. This was remarked upon by Jane and Louise Wilson in an interview with Lisa Corrin of the Serpentine Gallery, London: "Imagine that the era of the Cold War is also the era of the space program—an extension of Cold War politics, conflict and competition. Think about the incongruity between challenging and conquering outer space but not being able to traverse one's street. Psychologically it was a kind of zero gravity."

Photographs such as *Skarfandry* (2000) and *Cosmonaut Suits* (2000) are more obvious references in the Wilson's work to the conquest of space. The image depicted in *Skarfandry* features three empty space suits lying prostrate in a wooden cabinet. The outfits look as if they have had the life sucked out of them and are reminders that the cosmonauts who once filled them, and their American counterparts, were soldiers in the Cold War. The empty suits recall the political violence of the space race.

Top and right: Børre Sæthre, *My Private Sky—Explosion Suite*, 2001. *Explosion Suite* consists of four corridors linked together to form a square. Each corridor has a row of window-like monitors playing a video loop of slow-motion explosions. Each monitor plays the same piece of footage but at a different time. The corridors are of similar length and decor, which adds to the sense of disorientation. The experience can be likened to walking along a passageway in an imaginary spacecraft and witnessing the destruction of a distant planet—a planet the spacecraft might be fleeing.

Top: Jane and Louise Wilson, *Cosmonaut Suits*, 2000. C-print mounted on aluminum. 180 x 180 cm. Edition of 4.

Cosmonauts and astronauts underwent all kinds of physical and psychological torture to ensure they were reliable enough to send into space. One of the procedures used in the training of a space walker involved sealing him in a cramped chamber for hours on end, then placing a hood over his head, taking him up in an airplane and throwing him out with a parachute. This was to ensure that the shock between the tight confines of a space capsule and the vast expanse of outer space would not induce panic or hysteria. Each retired spacesuit in the picture was once a highly engineered component of the grand experiment to send humans into space. They are now arranged within a confined space formed by a wooden shelving unit. The repetitive stacking of the shelves echoes the rigid order of the old Soviet system. One of the shelves is without a spacesuit, but contains a few other pieces of kit. Maybe this cosmonaut did not make it back in one piece? The image is claustrophobic, tomb-like, and deathly.

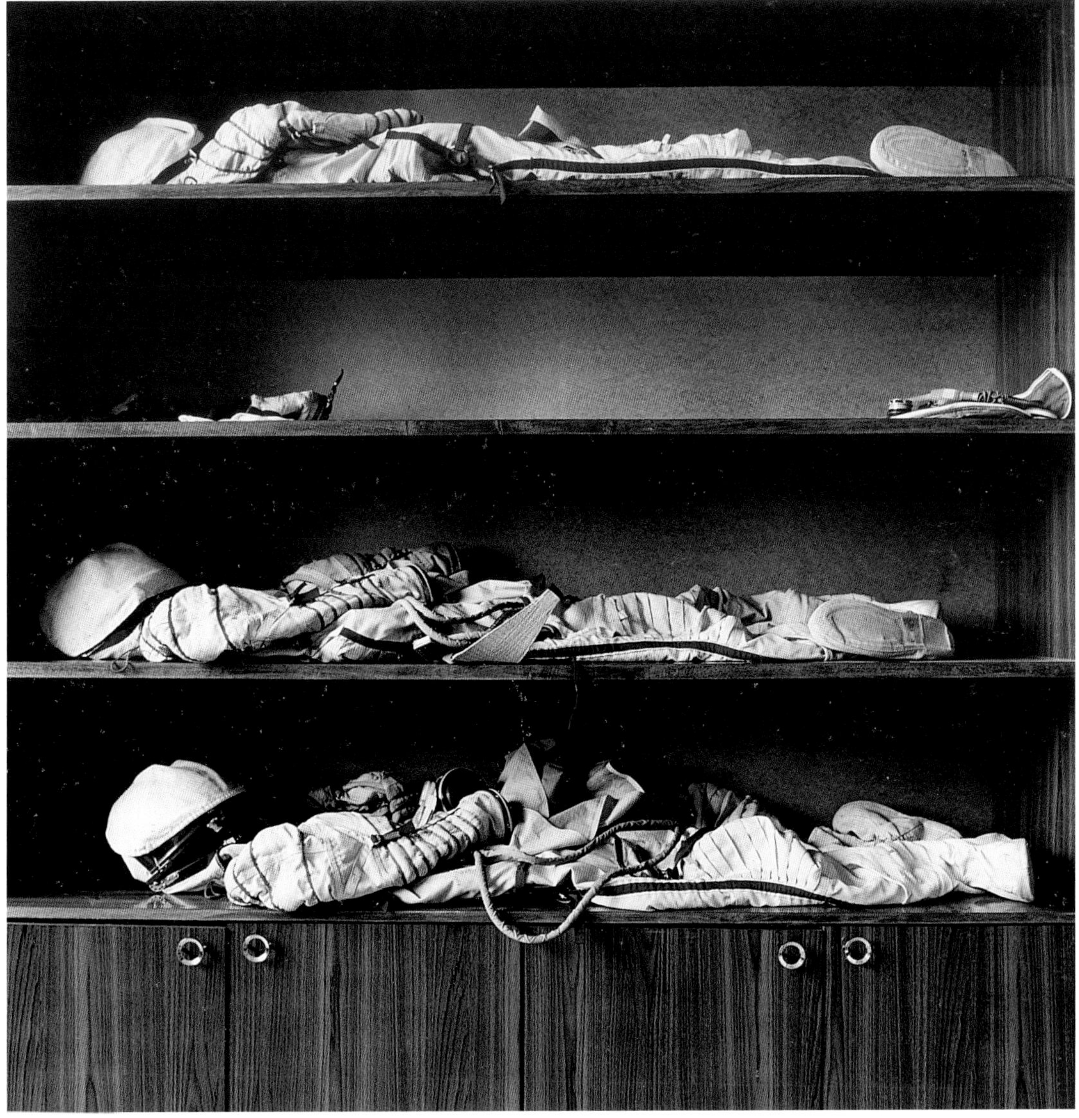

Cosmonaut Suits features two cosmonauts holding themselves up on Zimmer frames. The room looks like some kind of training facility and contains a circular hatch, rails, hoses, and other machinery in the background. The suits are obviously very heavy to lift in normal gravity. The cosmonauts might look magical and dynamic in the weightless conditions of space, but on earth they seem clumsy and sluggish. A pair of curtains frame the image like a theater stage and reminds us we are watching a performance.

The heroic images of astronauts and cosmonauts in space have been subverted by Jane and Louise Wilson into inert, empty shells. The identity of the USSR is inextricably linked to space travel. The communist superpower made its name through its achievements in space and for a while had America on the ropes. The Wilsons' work is a reminder that behind the thrilling veneer of the conquest of space there was enough destructive power to annihilate the world.

Top: Jane and Louise Wilson, *Skarfandry*, 2000. C-print mounted on aluminum. 180 x 180 cm. Edition of 4.

04 Conclusion

It is over thirty years since the last Apollo mission departed the lunar surface, but many of us are still trying to make sense of the incredible events that defined the space age. Art and culture have always reflected the public's mixed emotions, some remaining in awe of the achievements, while others are repulsed by the motivation behind the cosmic spectacle and question the results of technological progress. Rocket science was explained to the public at large in best-selling books and the battle to conquer space became a critical issue for political leaders on both sides of the Iron Curtain. Picture magazines carried features on the home lives of genuine spacemen and delivered the cosmos to the coffee table. Then came transmissions from outer space: first the distinctive beeps of the Sputnik satellite, then, with the blurry TV pictures of Neil Armstrong stepping onto the moon, the space age made its way into the living rooms of millions. However, that was a step too far for some. In many ways the space age made children of everybody: zero gravity in space brought a ground zero of knowledge on the earth, as we had to accept our insignificant place in the universe.

The space age entered the home as a child's plaything, but from the toy box it threatened to take over the whole house. The new discoveries in space were like a child learning about its own immediate environment for the very first time. When the cosmonauts and astronauts took their first steps in space they were able to share those experiences with the rest of mankind in a way a robotic probe never could. Outer space was a brand new playground, but the few who lost their lives reminded all the onlookers that it was not a game. The conquest of space demanded a break from tradition, and designers of all kinds leapt at the opportunity to define exactly what constituted the space-age home. The formality of the past was pushed aside as designers envisaged a domestic environment where comfort and relaxation ruled. Sharp corners gave way to soft curves and precious materials to affordable plastics. The new trend for capsule living mirrored the confines of the spacecraft in orbit around the earth, but the stark cleanliness of the condensed interiors was far removed from the mess of wires that filled the real space capsules. Mobility and adaptability were celebrated everywhere from architecture to fashion. New outfits embraced synthetic materials and